MODERN
NATIONS
—OF THE—
WORLD

ENGLAND

MODERN
NATIONS
—OF THE—
WORLD

ENGLAND

BY WILLIAM W. LACE

LUCENT BOOKS
P.O. BOX 289011
SAN DIEGO, CA 92198-9011

Library of Congress Cataloging-in-Publication Data

Lace, William W.
     England / by William W. Lace.
          p.   cm. — (Modern nations of the world)
     Includes bibliographical references and index.
     Summary: Examines the land, history, and people of England and
discusses its state of affairs and place in the world today.
     ISBN 1-56006-194-4 (alk. paper)
     1. England—Juvenile literature.   [1. England.]   I. Title. II. Series.
DA27.5.L33   1997
942—dc21   96-40121
                                                                          CIP
                                                                           AC

Copyright © 1997 by Lucent Books, Inc.
P.O. Box 289011, San Diego, CA 92198-9011
Printed in the U.S.A.

CONTENTS

INTRODUCTION

"THIS SCEPTER'D ISLE"

England is not large, as countries go. Its land area would rank twenty-eighth among the United States—larger than North Carolina and only slightly smaller than Alabama. A motorist can start out from Nottingham, roughly in the center of England, and easily reach any part of the country in a single day's drive.

England is the principal country of four that make up the United Kingdom of Great Britain and Northern Ireland. She was once the mightiest nation on earth militarily, but is no longer. Her armed forces were weakened by World War I and depleted by World War II. She never entered the post-war arms race and fell far behind the superpowers—the United States, the Soviet Union, and the People's Republic of China.

ONCE AT THE TOP

England was once the world's supreme political power, but is no longer. English influence made and toppled kings and presidents. Now, England's leading role on the world stage has been reduced to that of a supporting player.

England was once the richest of all nations, but is no longer. Her colonial empire disappeared bit by bit in the decades after World War II and with it went much of her wealth. London was replaced as the financial capital of the world by New York and Tokyo. England still is counted among the major industrialized nations, but her per capita income is now less than that of France and Italy.

The importance of England lies not in what she is, however, but rather in what she was. This small island nation, for centuries considered a barbaric outpost on the extreme edge of civilization, emerged from more than a century of foreign and civil wars in the Middle Ages and rose to a position of prominence, then dominance. From that position, England had an influence on the world greater than any na-

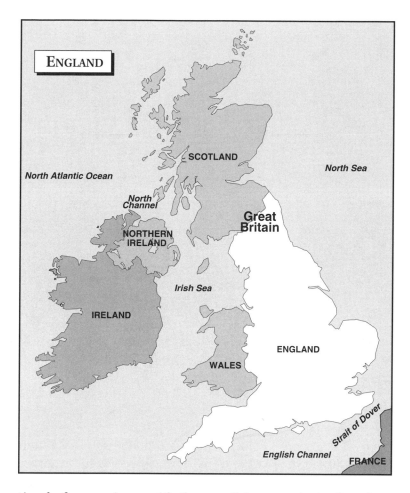

tion before or since, with the possible exceptions of ancient Greece and Rome.

William Shakespeare, in *Richard II*, called England "this precious stone set in the silver sea." At its greatest, England was indeed like a finely cut diamond reflecting the light of her culture to almost every corner of the globe. As the flag of Great Britain was planted around the world, English traditions followed, took root, and flourished. Maharajahs in India, kings in Africa, and chieftains in the Americas sent their sons to English universities. These sons returned home to rule with English ideas and ideals.

THE UNIVERSAL LANGUAGE

Thus it is that English most closely approaches a universal language. In virtually every country where English is not a

The Houses of Parliament stretch along the edge of the Thames River. Parliamentary governments around the world have used English law as their model.

native language, it is the one most studied in schools. When the Korean airline pilot talks with the air traffic controller in Rome, they speak English.

The spread of English has led to a corresponding spread of English literature. Shakespeare is the best known, most widely read writer in history. Authors and playwrights, not only in England but also in the United States, Canada, and Australia, have made English the largest contributor to world literature.

Likewise, the legal system of much of the world is based on English common law, in which justice is administered by professional judges using tradition as their guiding principle. Even the trappings of the English legal system have been copied around the world. The judge in Nairobi may wear the same style of long horsehair wig as does the judge in London. And most systems rely on juries, an English invention.

English governmental traditions and institutions are to be found everywhere. Parliaments around the world are modeled on the English Parliament, even when they go by another name, such as the Knesset of Israel. The legislative bodies of the U.S. government and most American states are, like Parliament, divided into two houses. The system of political parties, common to most countries, began in England.

THE CHURCH OF ENGLAND

Along with English law and government has come English religion. When King Henry VIII broke from the Roman Catholic Church in 1534, he established more than the Church of England. His new church would grow into the various denominations known collectively as Anglican that now claim more than 90 million members worldwide.

In addition to its tangible contributions to culture and society, England has always had a strong appeal to the imagination. In England the legendary King Arthur and the authentic Richard the Lionheart did their valiant deeds, and Henry VIII proposed to and disposed of several wives. It is a land of castles and cricket, of Buckingham Palace and the Beatles—a country where the past and the present coexist, where buildings a thousand years old are tarnished with today's factory smoke. It is England, with her glorious past and uncertain future.

1

THE LAND

The most important geographical fact about England, one that has profoundly affected its history, character, and culture, is that it is an island, or rather, part of an island. It is located on the largest of several islands that make up the British Isles, which lie just off the European mainland, across the English Channel from France and across the North Sea from Belgium and the Netherlands. Thus the English have always considered themselves somewhat removed and have stood aloof from the rest of Europe, even though they are separated by only about twenty miles of water.

A TEMPERATE CLIMATE

England occupies the southern portion of Britain, bounded by Wales on the west and Scotland on the north, and covers 50,363 square miles. Its northerly location—the English city of Berwick is at about the same latitude as Copenhagen; Moscow; and Juneau, Alaska—would seem to indicate a cold climate, but warm water and air currents carried by the Gulf Stream across the Atlantic Ocean from the Caribbean Sea give England a temperate climate. London's average temperature is thirty-nine degrees Fahrenheit in January and sixty-three degrees Fahrenheit in July.

Temperatures remain in a fairly narrow range. Highs in the summer only rarely reach ninety degrees, which is fortunate since air conditioning is very limited. Likewise, there is little bitterly cold weather. Snow is frequent, especially in the northern mountains, but tends to fall in moderate amounts and to melt rapidly. A white Christmas in London is very rare, despite images to the contrary projected in Charles Dickens's tale of Ebenezer Scrooge and Tiny Tim.

Rainfall is also moderate in England. Because of the moist winds blowing from the Atlantic, the western part of the country receives the most rainfall. Penzance in the far southwest averages 42 inches per year and Keswick in the northwest 58 inches. On the other hand, London in the east

Although England enjoys a temperate climate, frequent, brief rainfalls are not uncommon. Here, English fans peer from beneath umbrellas as they wait for the start of a tennis match.

receives an average of 23 inches and Dover on the east coast 33 inches.

England's reputation for dampness rests with the frequency of rain, not the volume. Most of the rain falls between October and January, but light, brief showers are a near daily occurrence even in the warmest summer months. Any area of England that goes three weeks without rain is officially in a drought.

Opinions of English weather have always varied, usually depending on the individual's viewpoint. The Roman historian Tacitus described it as "objectionable, with frequent rains and mists." Tacitus, however, was from sunny Italy. English king Charles II, on the other hand, boasted that "a man can enjoy outdoor exercises in all but five days of the year."

England can be roughly divided into two topographic zones. If a line is drawn from the northeast to the southwest, everything east of the line generally will be the lowlands and everything west the highlands. Highlands, however, is a relative term. The highest point in England, Scafell Pike, is only 3,210 feet above sea level. Only in Wales to the west and Scotland to the north are true mountains to be found.

Britain was once part of the European landmass. A land bridge connected France and Britain until about 5000 B.C., when the great glaciers melted and the seas rose, cutting Britain off from the rest of Europe. A topographic map of

A view of London's Westminster Bridge by night shows Big Ben and the Houses of Parliament in the background.

Europe demonstrates how the British Isles are an extension of the mainland. The mountains of Norway, the highlands of Scotland, and the highlands of western Ireland form a straight line and were once part of the same range. Similarly, the marshy lowlands of East Anglia are much like those of the Netherlands that lie just a few miles across the sea. In fact, if Britain were to slide to the east it would fit into mainland Europe almost like a puzzle piece.

Although England can be crudely divided into two sections, the land and vegetation within each section vary dramatically. Indeed, there is far more variety of landscape than would normally be found in so relatively small a space. A cross-country drive of only a few hours can encompass marshes, rolling hills, dense forests, mountains, and barren moors. It is as if the diverse terrains that stretch for hundreds of miles in other countries have been squeezed together in England.

LONDON

Almost any discussion of England, whether about government, culture, trade, or geography, begins with London, the capital city so large as to be a geographical region in itself. The London known to tourists is only a small part of Greater London, which covers almost eight hundred square miles. London is built in a basin fifty miles wide on either side of the Thames River, about one hundred miles inland from the sea.

LIVING FENCES

One of the most charming aspects of the English landscape are fences, some more than a thousand years old, that surround fields and meadows. They are not made of stone or wire, but have been planted, grown, and maintained over the centuries. These living fences are called hedgerows.

The first hedgerows were "planted" in England by Anglo-Saxon settlers, who had erected similar fences in their European homelands. They were used to mark the limits of a village's territory, to fence in livestock, or as a defense against attack. Most Anglo-Saxon hedges were "dead" hedges, with hawthorn branches woven throughout a series of stakes planted in the ground.

The trouble with dead hedges was that they required constant repair. Around the time of the Norman invasion in 1066, dead hedges began to be replaced with "live" or "quick" hedges consisting of living hawthorn trees either raised from seeds or transplanted.

Live hedges took many years to grow. At first, it was necessary to reinforce them with stakes and woven hazel branches. With time, however, the hawthorns grew to be tightly bunched, their thorns serving to keep any animals from pushing through.

Over time, seeds from other plants were carried by the wind into the hedges and other species took root, grew, and made the hedge even stronger. Trees such as oak, ash, and elm sprang up, and were used for firewood and building. Flowers and herbs grew at the base of the hedge and were harvested for medicines. Experts can date a hedge by the number of different trees and plants it contains.

Live hedgerows required annual maintenance. Some bushes and trees died and had to be replaced. Most important for the Norman landowners was that hedgerows had to be kept trimmed at about the height of a man's shoulder, high enough to keep livestock in but short enough to see over and for a horse to jump over during hunting.

Ancient hedgerows create living fences that divide the English landscape.

Because the Thames provides easy access to mainland Europe, it was a natural site for a port. Although there were a few earlier settlements nearby, London was first built by the Romans in the first century A.D. on some of the gravel-topped hills rising out of the marshy riverbank. These firm spots in the marshes gave names to some areas of London, such as Chelsea and Battersea, "ea" in the old Saxon language meaning "island."

East of London, the land becomes flatter and more marshy as the Thames winds its way to the sea. West of the city, however, the land rises toward the Chiltern Hills, and forests of beech and birch trees begin to appear. In addition to Greater London, the Thames Valley takes in large parts of the counties of Buckinghamshire and Berkshire, and the suburbs of London reach well into Surrey, Essex, and Hertfordshire, as well.

Beyond the Chilterns is Oxfordshire, a county located almost entirely in the Thames Basin. The clay soil of the lowlands is good for growing grass and feed grains for cattle, and Oxfordshire is a center of beef production. The limestone hills in the north and southwest provide pasture for sheep. Mining yields ironstone, clay, and various gravels.

SOUTH AND SOUTHEAST

The most pleasant climate in England and some of the best farming is found in the region fanning south from London comprising the counties of Kent, Surrey, East and West Sussex, and Hampshire. Running east to west through the middle of southeastern England is the Weald, a dome of sandstone sloping down to lowlands of clay soil on either side.

Portions of the Wealden Dome are heavily wooded with stands of ash, hazel, chestnut, and oak trees, remnants of the great Forest of Andred that once covered the entire region. Indeed, most of England was once covered with forests so vast that it was said that a squirrel could go the length or width of the country without touching the ground. Over the centuries, however, the forests have slowly disappeared—cleared for agriculture, cut down for fuel, or, as in the Weald, used for shipbuilding.

The lowlands of the Weald, with their rich soil and mild climate, are sometimes called "the orchard of England." Apples, pears, and cherries are major crops, along with hops—flowers that when dried are an important ingredient in brewing beer

ARTWORKS IN CHALK

The landscape in many parts of England features downs, or hills, composed of chalk covered by a thin layer of topsoil and grass. The people of ancient Britain and their descendants over the centuries have used this form of nature to fashion art.

It was the Iberians who first saw the possibility of scraping away the topsoil and vegetation to expose the white chalk in such a manner as to form gigantic pictographs on the sides of the hills. It is not known whether these figures served any purpose, but scientists have speculated that they may have been objects of worship or may have served to mark or identify the territory of individual tribes.

The oldest chalk figure is the White Horse of Uffington a few miles southwest of Oxford. Despite legends that it was carved by the Saxon chief Hengist, whose name means "stallion" in German, the figure is much older. Hengist is thought to have come to England in about A.D. 450. Experts have dated the White Horse, which measures about 350 feet from nose to tail, at about 3000 B.C.

Horses were a popular subject for chalk figures, but humans were also pictured. Near the village of Cerne Abbas in Wessex is a 180-foot-tall giant holding what appears to be a club. He is thought to be a two-thousand-year-old picture of an Iron Age warrior. Another curiously proportioned human figure near the town of Lewes in Sussex is named the Long Man.

There was a revival of interest in chalk figures in the 1700s, and many new carvings were made in hillsides all over England. Most have now been overgrown, but one that remains is a huge white horse near Sutton Bank in North Yorkshire. Chalk figures require periodic maintenance called "scouring" to prevent grass from overgrowing them.

The chalk figures carved into English hillsides have intrigued visitors for thousands of years.

and ale. One of the distinctive features of Kent are the oast houses, kilns with cone-shaped towers where hops are dried.

On either side of the Weald are ranges of chalk hills known as "downs" from an old Anglo-Saxon word for hill. The North Downs stretch from eastern Hampshire and run south of Greater London to the Strait of Dover. The South Downs follow the southern coast of England through Hampshire and Sussex. The gently rolling downs look as if they would be

A ferry carrying tourists passes by the magnificent chalk cliffs of Dover.

ideal for farming, but the soil is thin and poor. The grass covering the downs, however, is ideal for sheep.

Along much of the southeastern shoreline, the downs end abruptly in spectacular chalk cliffs, the most famous of which are the white cliffs of Dover. In other places, however, the land slopes down to the shore and forms long, sandy beaches. Such coastal towns as Eastbourne and Brighton are favorite vacation destinations for the English.

East Anglia

Northeast of London is East Anglia, the most unusual region of England. Comprising the counties of Essex, Suffolk, Norfolk, and Cambridgeshire, East Anglia features a low, flat, often waterlogged countryside that seems much more like the Netherlands than part of Britain. Indeed, one particularly marshy section is known as the Parts of Holland.

Historically, East Anglia was one of England's most remote regions, not because of distance from London, but because of inaccessibility. Roads were few, and the numerous marshes, lakes, and rivers made getting from place to place extremely difficult. Those who wanted solitude, either criminals hiding from the law or monks retreating from worldly pursuits, found it in East Anglia. Towns and cities were built on spots of higher ground that were virtually islands.

Prehistoric people built houses above the marshes on poles and used stilts to move about the land, catching birds and gathering reeds for building material. Roman conquerors began the job of draining the marshes for farmland, and the task has continued into this century. Today, much of the land has been converted from swamps into plowland on which wheat and potatoes, among other crops, are grown and into pasturage for sheep. Water still plays an important role in the area's economy, however; freshwater and saltwater fishing are major sources of income.

Most of the soil is a combination of chalk and clay with the notable exception of the Breckland, an area straddling the Norfolk-Suffolk border that has a sandy soil not found in other parts of the country. Another unique feature of East Anglia is the Norfolk Broads, where centuries of cutting peat moss has created a series of wide rivers and lagoons, a favorite place for both fishing and boating.

THE MIDLANDS

North of East Anglia and running from the North Sea on the east to the Welsh border on the west is the large area known as the Midlands. It is usually thought of as two regions. The East Midlands comprises Lincolnshire, Nottinghamshire, Derbyshire, Leicestershire, and Northamptonshire. Seven counties—Avon, Staffordshire, Cheshire, Salop, Hereford and Worcester, Warwickshire, Gloucestershire and Avon—make up the West Midlands.

The East Midlands is a diverse area containing some of England's best farmland, richest coalfields, and largest areas of forest. The landscape also is varied: Eastern Lincolnshire is low, flat, and marshy, much like East Anglia. The land rises farther to the west, and northwestern Derbyshire contains the Peak District, a southern extension of the Pennine Chain that, because of its wonderful scenic views, is a favorite with hikers. In between can be found chalk hills, clay lowlands, limestone ridges, and forests.

Generally, agriculture is more important in the eastern portion of the East Midlands. Sugar beets, grains, and vegetables are grown in Lincolnshire and Nottinghamshire, areas also famous for their dairy products, particularly the pungent Stilton cheese. Farther west lie the large deposits of coal and iron that made the East Midlands towns centers of industry and manufacturing. Leicester, for instance, is known for hosiery and shoes and Derby for automobiles.

THE COUNTIES OF ENGLAND

Perhaps the best-known natural feature of the East Midlands is Sherwood Forest. Occupying an area of rocky soil north of Nottingham, Sherwood still features stands of mighty oak trees. As in other parts of England, however, most of the vast wood in which Robin Hood and his Merry Men supposedly lived has disappeared.

THE WEST MIDLANDS

The West Midlands contains the best and worst of England. The best includes the beautiful Cotswold Hills in the south, dotted with picturesque villages of thatched-roof houses built of soft, golden Cotswold stone. The worst includes the so-called Black Country—the heavily industrialized northern cities such as Birmingham, Manchester, and Stoke-on-Trent with their stark skylines and rows of bleak, soot-stained houses and apartments.

Throughout much of England's history, the southern and western parts of the West Midlands were more heavily populated than the north. Agriculture has always been important, and the reddish soil, rich in iron, produces good crops of grain and fruits and the grass to support a thriving dairy industry. To the west, Hereford and Worcester ranks second in hops production only to Kent and also produces pears and cider apples. Both dairy and beef cattle are raised, the latter mostly the famous white-faced Hereford breed.

Many of England's remaining forests are found in the southern West Midlands. The Forest of Dean, once exclusively the hunting grounds of royalty, is now a national park covering about forty square miles. Some of the region's oak trees are among the oldest in the country, and there are also great stands of beeches.

The northern part of the West Midlands remained heavily wooded and sparsely settled until the 1700s, when discovery of abundant deposits of iron and coal led to the birth and growth of the steel industry and heavy manufacturing. During the Industrial Revolution of the 1800s, the villages of the northern West Midlands swelled to great, grimy urban centers. It was called the Black Country, because the factory smoke and coal dust turned everything—buildings, vegetation, the sky—a dingy gray. The forests that once covered the hills were either cut down for fuel or killed off by pollution.

Today, modern pollution controls and government regulation have partially restored the landscape. There is less mining than before, but the area remains the most important industrial region of England.

THE WEST COUNTRY

South of the Midlands and west of London lies the area known as the West Country, which includes the counties of Wiltshire, Somerset, Dorset, Devon, and Cornwall. The region contains some of the most varied landscapes and the most striking scenery in England.

The eastern counties are dominated by chalk uplands, and the Salisbury Plain in Wiltshire is the closest thing in England to a prairie. Its broad, open spaces have long provided a site for military maneuvers, including those by American troops in World War II. Between the ridges of chalk hills are lowlands with a mixture of clay and sandy soils ideal for grain crops, mainly barley. Dairy farming is a major industry, and the area is well known for its cheeses, especially the famous Cheddar. The English poultry industry is also centered here.

The westernmost counties of Devon and Cornwall are very different geologically from their neighbors. Large granite formations in Devon have created the high plateaus known as moors—rough hills on which few trees grow and only coarse grasses and heather provide ground cover. Two moors—Exmoor and Dartmoor—have been set aside as national parks.

Cornwall is as distinctive in its own way as is East Anglia. Moor-topped granite formations are also found here, and a

ST. MICHAEL'S MOUNT

An unusual geographical phenomenon at almost the southwestern tip of England has been put to use by humans for almost two thousand years. Within the curve of Mount Bay on the southern coast of Cornwall a rocky hill less than a mile across rises out of the water.

Most of the time it is an island. At low tide, however, one can cross a cobblestone causeway to the mainland about four hundred yards away. In Roman times, the place was called the island of Ictis and was a port where ships from all over the ancient world came to load Cornish tin.

The Normans noted its resemblance to a similar island off the coast of France called Mont-Saint-Michel and named the English version Mount St. Michael. It was given to the Benedictine monks of the abbey of Mont-Saint-Michel, who sent some of their order to build a sister abbey on the new site.

The monastery was dissolved in the 1500s when Henry VIII broke with the Roman Catholic Church, and the building was turned into a fortress, one of a series along England's southern coast to defend against possible attack from France.

In 1659, Mount St. Michael was purchased by Sir John St. Aubyn, who began the building of a magnificent house atop the hill. His descendants still live there.

Mount St. Michael

geologically recent rise in sea level has flooded several coastal river valleys, creating numerous inlets and coves lined by rocks against which the surf crashes. Surrounded on three sides by the sea, Cornwall has the wettest, windiest weather in England.

In ancient times, Devon and Cornwall were the most important mining areas, chiefly for tin. Today, the land is mostly used for agriculture, primarily dairy cattle.

The westernmost county of Cornwall endures more rain and wind than any other English county, but it also boasts some of the most beautiful coastal scenery in England.

THE NORTH

Above the Midlands is the large region that throughout much of English history has been known simply as "the North." The North can be divided into three general areas: Yorkshire-Humberside, Lancashire-Cumbria, and Durham-Northumberland. Geographically remote, economically poor, sparsely populated, the North traditionally played a minor role in the affairs of the kingdom. That changed with the Industrial Revolution, and the North is now an important contributor to the English economy.

Yorkshire was formerly the largest county in England but now has been divided into three counties—North, West, and South Yorkshire. The western parts of the region are dominated by the Pennine mountains, the "backbone of

The picturesque Lake District in Cumbria lures visitors from around the world.

England" that runs from the Scottish border down the middle of the country to the Midlands. Cutting through the mountains are deep river valleys known as dales. Far to the east is an upland area of limestone and sandstone forming the extensive Yorkshire moors, a large, barren area on which grows coarse grasses good only for sheep.

Between the uplands and the mountains, the Vale of York has soil fertile enough to grow much of England's grain. Dairy farming also is a major industry. To the southeast, Humberside's economy is based on the Humber River and its deepwater channel that extends twenty-two miles inland. Kingston-upon-Hull is a fishing center and one of England's major ports.

West of the Pennines are Lancashire and Cumbria. Cumbria is generally considered the most scenic county in England because of its Lake District, an area of mountain peaks and deep, lake-filled valleys just west of the mountains. The highest peaks in England are found in far eastern Cumbria. Most of the land is fit only for sheep, but there is some farming in the Cheshire Basin.

Lancashire, to the south of Cumbria, also has a highland section on the western flank of the Pennines that falls to moors in the central portion and then to the lowlands alongside the Irish Sea. Beef and dairy cattle are raised in the north, and the major ports of Lancaster, Liverpool, and Preston line its coast.

The wildest, most unspoiled region of England is the far north, for centuries a battleground between the English and invaders from Scotland. As with many other areas of the north, the geography is dictated by the Pennines. Both major counties—Durham and Northumberland—slope from the mountains eastward to the North Sea. Rivers cut through the hills, and farming is possible in the valleys, but most of the land is used for sheep grazing. In the west, towns are few and far between. Western Northumberland is the least-populated part of England and is separated from Scotland on the north by the Chevoit Hills.

The eastern parts of Durham and Northumberland differ from the west and from each other. Dairy farming predominates in eastern Durham, but the eastern portion of Northumberland is a center of heavy industry, thanks mostly to plentiful rich deposits of coal west of the city of Newcastle, giving rise to the expression "like carrying coals to Newcastle" to mean giving something to a person who already has plenty of it.

The seemingly endless variety of English landscapes and their compactness are sources of constant amazement to tourists, particularly Americans accustomed to prairies, mountain ranges, and forests measured in hundreds of square miles. This variety has been very beneficial to the English people, however, permitting a diversity of economy that would be impossible in a country more geographically unified.

2

THE PEOPLE

Most people have a mental picture of the "typical" English-man or Englishwoman. To some, it may be the dark-suited businessman hurrying through London with bowler hat and umbrella. To others, it may be the Yorkshire farmwife, the very proper retired colonel, the London flower seller, or even the punk rocker with purple and orange hair. England encompasses all of these and more. The people of England are the product of an ongoing mixture of ethnic groups that has been occurring for thousands of years. The result is a population almost as diverse as the landscape.

Geography has played a major role in the settlement of England and in the diversity of its people. Successive waves of invaders sweeping across the island over the centuries sometimes assimilated the people they conquered. At other times, however, the conquered peoples were pushed back into the more remote areas of Britain. There, in relative isolation, they developed unique customs and cultures.

Thousands of years before Britain was separated from Europe, Stone Age hunters and their families wandered across the land bridge in search of game. Although several tribes migrated to Britain over many centuries, these people are known collectively as the Iberians. Slowly, the Iberians turned from hunting to agriculture, clearing small areas in the huge forests and gradually spreading into every corner of the island. As they grew more settled, they erected monuments that survive today, such as the famous ring of stones known as Stonehenge.

THE CELTS

The next major addition to the population came with the invasion of the Celts, which began about 700 B.C. and lasted four hundred years. In contrast to the Iberians, who were a short, dark-skinned people, the Celts were tall and fair. There were many tribes of Celts, including the Gaels, who gave their name to Gaelic, the language still spoken in some remote sections of Britain and Ireland. Also among the Celts were the Cymri—the Welsh word today for Wales is Cymru—and the Brythons, from whom the name Britain is derived.

As the Celts advanced, those Iberians who were not assimilated fled into Scotland, Wales, and Cornwall or crossed the sea to Ireland. Only in these isolated, often mountainous areas were they safe from pursuit and left to themselves. The results can still be seen. The people of these regions are generally darker skinned and shorter than those in the rest of Britain, reflecting their Iberian heritage.

The Celts were technologically far more advanced than the Iberians, using iron tools instead of stone or bronze and minting gold coins. Their religion was based on nature worship and was presided over by priests called Druids who practiced human sacrifice. The Celts were by no means a unified people. The various tribes were constantly at war with one another, painting themselves with a blue dye called woad before battle.

THE ROMANS

Eventually the Celts of England had a common enemy—the legions of the Roman Empire. Celtic tribes in Gaul (modern-day France and Belgium) had been at war against Roman troops led by the famous general Julius Caesar and had

Roman ships approach the rugged shores of England. The Romans' four-hundred-year occupation of Britain would leave an indelible mark on the history of England. One of the Romans' lasting contributions to England was the introduction of Christianity.

been receiving help from their cousins in Britain. In retaliation, Caesar mounted expeditions against Britain in 55 and 54 B.C., both of which failed. It was not until the next century that Rome, under the emperor Claudius, conquered Britain and made it a Roman colony.

The Romans occupied Britain for four hundred years. Unlike the Celts before them, they were able to conquer Wales and keep the population under control with a system of forts and roads over which troops could be moved quickly. They were never able to conquer Scotland, however; instead, in A.D. 123 Emperor Hadrian ordered a wall built across the island to keep out the wild tribes of Picts, Scots, and Caledonians. The wall, parts of which still exist, extended seventy-three miles and was studded with garrisons of Roman soldiers. The Romans made no attempt to conquer Ireland.

The Romans changed the face of England. They built cities that became centers of trade, including London, York, Gloucester, Colchester, and Lincoln. The land became peaceful. The Celts still in England adopted Roman customs, wearing togas and living in villas, content to leave the security of the country to the Roman legions.

Shortly after 400 Rome itself was threatened by Germanic tribes such as the Vandals and Goths. Its empire crumbling, in 410 Rome withdrew its legions from Britain. Despite its long tenure in England, Roman civilization would leave few lasting marks. One was in the names of cities, many of which still include the suffix -*caster* or -*chester*, from the Latin word for fort. The greater contribution of Rome was Christianity, well established on the island by missionaries and strong enough to survive the next invasion.

THE ANGLO-SAXONS

The departure of the Romans left Britain defenseless. The Celts hired warriors from Europe to fight their northern enemies. Unfortunately, these warriors liked the country so well they decided to invade it themselves. Three tribes—the Angles, Saxons, and Jutes—came to England in waves and—despite a great victory supposedly won by the Celts under King Arthur, took over England within a century. The Celts were pushed into the remote parts of the island just as they had displaced the Iberians.

The Anglo-Saxons, as they are generally known, had little use for the Romanized civilization they conquered. Cities dwindled to villages or were abandoned altogether. The Anglo-Saxons were farmers, fishermen, and sometimes pirates. They were the first of several ethnic groups to be seafarers. They came across the North Sea from their homelands in Denmark and northwestern Germany and by 550 had settled all modern-day England except for Cornwall. The Saxons settled in the south, the Jutes in the southeast, and the Angles, from which England —"Angle-Land"—took its name, in the east and north. As the

HENGIST AND HORSA

When the Roman legions left Britain in A.D. 410, the British tribes who had lived peaceably under Roman protection for almost four centuries were left on their own. Soon, they began to suffer raids from the north, as the Picts, Scots, and Caledonians swept across the abandoned wall that had been built in the second century by the emperor Hadrian.

The Britons had once been warlike but had grown soft under Roman rule and were unable to defend themselves. Sometime around 450, the British king Vortigern invited two brothers, Hengist and Horsa, to bring their followers from their home in what was probably northwest Germany, to help him fight off the invaders.

The brothers landed in Kent in southeast England and never returned to their own country. Some accounts say they were so impressed with England that they decided on their own to stay and began what turned out to be the Anglo-Saxon invasion. Other stories say that Vortigern, as payment for their help, gave Hengist and Horsa the kingdom of Kent.

Shortly thereafter, Vortigern realized his mistake and war broke out between the Britons and the newcomers. Horsa was killed about 455, but Hengist defeated the Britons in four great battles and was eventually granted dominion over the areas that came to be known as Essex and Sussex.

Although Vortigern has been established as a historical figure, there is no concrete proof that such persons as Hengist and Horsa existed. Nevertheless, the Anglo-Saxon kings of Kent who ruled until the 900s claimed to be descended from Hengist's son Oeric.

British king Vortigern greets Hengist and Horsa, whom he invited to help fight off foreign invaders.

invaders reached the Severn River in the southwest and the Mersey and Dee in the northwest, the Celtic sections of Britain—Cornwall, Wales, and Scotland—were cut off from one another and began to develop distinct cultures.

Although they built no cities, the Anglo-Saxons cleared the land for hundreds of small settlements separated from one another by the forest and surrounded by open fields divided into strips farmed by individual families. These settlements became villages, and the pattern of rural England—a network of open fields and villages with central market towns where people traded their goods—was established. The pattern would remain essentially unchanged for almost a thousand years.

The Anglo-Saxons were no more united than the Celts had been. They formed several small kingdoms constantly at war with one another. There were seven principal kingdoms: Wessex, Sussex, Essex (the kingdoms of the West Saxons, South Saxons, and East Saxons), Kent, East Anglia, Mercia, and Northumberland. Although agriculture was the

The Angles disembark to invade the English coast. After forcing the Celts into remote parts of England, the Angles, along with the Saxons and Jutes, would eventually create their own kingdom.

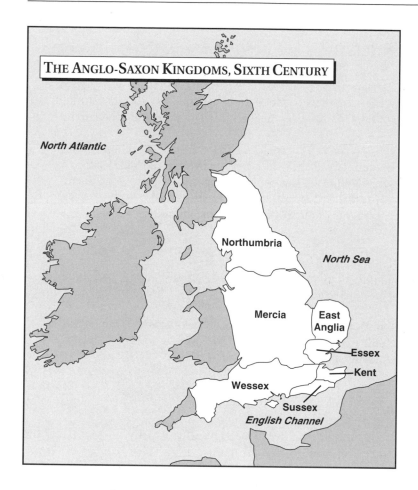

THE ANGLO-SAXON KINGDOMS, SIXTH CENTURY

North Atlantic

Northumbria

North Sea

Mercia

East Anglia

Essex

Kent

Wessex

Sussex

English Channel

basis of their economy, fighting was their chief pastime. The social ladder ascended from freemen (*ceorls*) to nobles (*ealdormen*) to the kings, who were believed to be descended from the gods. The nobles originally were the king's companions, warriors who had done him great service. Gradually, however, nobility became heritable and the rank was passed from father to children.

The Anglo-Saxons were a warrior people, and their religion reflected that fact. They worshiped the pagan gods of Scandinavia—Odin, Thor, Balder, and the rest. Their highest values were not compassion or humility, but rather bravery, generosity, and loyalty. There was only a vague idea of an afterlife. Altogether, it was an easygoing religion, which, when eventually combined with Christianity, produced a uniquely English blend.

EARLY ENGLISH

In the century following the Anglo-Saxon invasion of England, four Germanic dialects spoken by the conquering tribes slowly combined to form Old English, the earliest form of the language that now is one of the most spoken and most studied in the world. The old form of English, however, bears only a slight resemblance to the English of today.

Few examples of Old English remain. The Anglo-Saxons were mostly illiterate, and only with the coming of Christianity was there much of an attempt to make written records. Alfred the Great, who died in 900, was probably the first English king able to read and write. He personally translated many books from Latin, and this commentary on the sad state of learning from one of his works shows how much English has changed over the centuries:

Swa clæne hio wæs oofeallenu on Angelkynne oætte swioe feawe wæron behionan Humbre pe hiora oenunga cuoan understandan on Englisc, oooe furoum an ærendgewrit of Lædene on Englisc areccan.

Translated into modern English, this reads, "So clean was it fallen away in England that very few there were on this side of the Humber who could understand their service-books in English, or even translate a letter from Latin into English."

THE ENGLISH LANGUAGE

These latest invaders brought something more important than their religion—their language. The Angles, Saxons, and Jutes spoke four Germanic dialects. After they had settled in their new country, their four dialects combined to form the oldest form of English. The language is almost unrecognizable as English and would undergo many changes before reaching its present form. It retained a few words from the Celts and would add many more from later invaders, but more than half of all words in modern English are rooted in Anglo-Saxon. The Anglo-Saxons were largely illiterate, and few examples of Old English remain. The outstanding surviving work is the epic poem *Beowulf*, thought to have been written by a Christian monk sometime between 700 and 750.

The fact that there existed a Christian monk to write *Beowulf* was due to the next invasion of England, a peaceful one, for a change. In 597, a monk named Augustine, sent by the pope, head of the Roman Catholic Church, converted the English of Kent to Christianity. At about the same time,

Celtic missionaries came from Ireland to preach among the people of Northumberland. By about 650, all of England was Christian.

THE DANISH AND NORMAN INVASIONS

The next invasion of England was not peaceful. Warriors from Denmark and Norway began raiding the coast in 789 and about 850 began a full-scale invasion. Over the next twenty years, the "Danes," as the English called all Scandinavians, had conquered all of eastern and northern England. The advance of the Danes was finally stopped in 878 at the Battle of Edington by Alfred of Wessex, but they held on to the "Danelaw," as their section of the country was called. Although Alfred, later called "the Great," is generally acknowledged as the first king of England, it was his

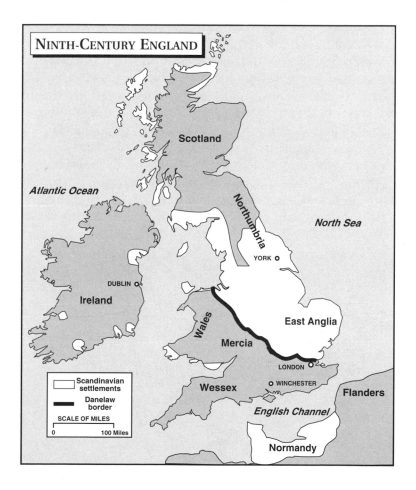

grandson, Athelstan, who finally conquered the Danes and was the first ruler of the entire country.

Even though the Danes were ultimately defeated, they remained in England in large numbers and had a lasting influence. For centuries, the people of northeast England were taller and blonder than their countrymen, reflecting Danish ancestry. English contains many words of Danish origin. Many cities and towns in the northeast end in the Danish -*by*, such as Derby, or -*thorpe*, as in Scunthorpe. In the south and west, place-names were more likely to end in the Anglo-Saxon -*tun* (town), -*ham* (home), or -*burgh* or -*borough* (fortified place).

THE BATTLE OF HASTINGS

The next, and last, successful invasion of England came in the year 1066 when William, duke of Normandy, landed an army on the southern coast and a few days later defeated the English king, Harold, at the Battle of Hastings. Although the Norman Conquest would have enormous social and political consequences, it had only a slight impact on the ethnic composition of the country. The Normans formed the ruling class, but they never came in great enough numbers to become a significant contributor to England's population.

The racial makeup of England was thus basically established by the year 1000. The Anglo-Saxon heritage is predominant, with Danish influence strong in the northeast and Celtic influence heavy in the far north and far west. The peopling of England from other countries, however,

The Battle of Hastings, depicted here on the Bayeux tapestry, pitted William, duke of Normandy, against the English king, Harold, in 1066.

THE BATTLE OF HASTINGS

Of all the battles in England or involving English armies or navies, none had more significance for the future of the country than did the Battle of Hastings in 1066. Three armies of about equal strength were struggling for control, and in the end it was only a change in the wind that decided the outcome.

The mother of Edward the Confessor, whose reign began in 1042, was from the French county of Normandy, and Edward vastly preferred Norman companions and customs to those of England. In 1052, the childless Edward named as his heir his cousin William, duke of Normandy. When Edward died in 1066, however, his chief adviser, Harold of Wessex, rejected William's claim and took the throne for himself. William immediately prepared to invade England.

There was a third rival for the crown. Harold Hardrada, king of Norway, had a claim based on an agreement his uncle, King Magnus, had once made with Harthacanute, who had been king of both Denmark and England from 1040 to 1042. As William prepared to invade from the south, Harold Hardrada, aided by King Harold's rebellious brother, Tostig, was readying his fleet to the north.

By midsummer, William was ready to sail, but steady winds from the north held him in port. Those same winds, however, allowed Harold Hardrada to sail from Norway in August, and his army landed in northeast England on September 15.

King Harold of England, who had been waiting for William's invasion, now had to march quickly northward with his army. At the Battle of Stamford Bridge on September 25, the English routed the Danes and Harold Hardrada and Tostig both were killed.

Two days after the battle, however, with Harold still away in the north, the wind shifted from north to south. William hurriedly loaded his ships and crossed the English Channel, landing at Pevensy. Harold and his exhausted, depleted army now had to rush back to counter this new threat. On October 14, after a fierce, day-long battle that could have gone either way, the English were defeated and Harold was killed. Had the wind changed only a week earlier, events might have been far different. A fresh English army might have defeated William, and then been defeated by Harold Hardrada. As it turned out, however, England, under Norman rule, became tied to France and southern Europe instead of becoming a Scandinavian country.

continued and still continues. In addition to the Normans, large numbers of Jews and French fleeing religious persecution came to England in the Middle Ages. There were large influxes from Ireland in the mid-1800s and from eastern Europe just before and during World War II. After World War II, great numbers of nonwhite people arrived from former British colonies in Africa, India, and the Caribbean. None, however, came in great enough numbers to have a large impact on the ethnic composition.

Today, more than 95 percent of England's population is of Anglo-Danish-Celtic origin. The largest ethnic minorities include Asian Indian (670,000, or 1.4 percent), Pakistani (430,000, or 0.9 percent), Caribbean and West Indian (382,000, or 0.8 percent), African (144,000, or 0.3 percent), Chinese (140,000, or 0.3 percent), Bangladeshi (95,000, or 0.2 percent), and Arab (48,000, or 0.1 percent).

Although nonwhites make up only about 4 percent of the total population, their impact has been greater than their numbers might indicate. They have become highly visible in the large cities. Manchester has a large Chinese section, and there are sizable Bangladeshi and Afro-Caribbean enclaves in East London.

Though England has a long history of assimilating the various peoples who have come to her shores, nonwhite, mostly poor immigrants have had a harder time than others. Most have settled in the poorer areas of the large cities, where they face competition from the poorer part of the white population for a shrinking number of jobs requiring little education or training. The resulting tensions have brought racial violence to a country where it had been virtually unknown.

THE TWO ENGLANDS

Although almost every town and village has an Indian restaurant or a Chinese-run convenience store, the vast majority of nonwhites—more than 90 percent—live in large cities. This has led to the formation of what is essentially two Englands. One consists of crowded, industrial, cosmopolitan cities in which people of many ethnic backgrounds work together, although not always in harmony. The other is the tourist picture of England—a rural country with fields and farms, bustling market towns, and quaint villages around every bend in the road.

The faces of the two Englands are reflected in the celebrations of the people. Festivals and fairs form an important part of English life, on themes great and small, from the annual Comedy Festival in Liverpool to the World Marble Championships in Tinsley Green to the yearly Grand Prix Power Lawnmower race in Wisborough Green.

Festivals in the more rural parts of the country revolve around agricultural and historical themes. The Goose Fair has been held in Nottingham for seven hundred years. York celebrates its Danish heritage with the Jorvick Festival. Queen Elizabeth II annually lends her backyard at Windsor Castle for the country's largest horse show. The summer months are packed with county fairs featuring stock shows, horse races, sheepdog and plowing competitions, and exhibitions of everything from boots to tractors.

For two days in the summer, however, Notting Hill looks more like Rio de Janeiro than a section of London as thousands of Caribbean immigrants put on a street carnival. Colorful Bangladeshi religious festivals are a major attraction in London's East End. Likewise, the Chinese New Year touches off major celebrations in Liverpool and Manchester.

Caribbean immigrants celebrate their heritage during a Notting Hill festival.

POPULATION SHIFTS

For most of its history, England was overwhelmingly rural. Except for London, which has long been one of Europe's largest cities, there were no metropolitan centers. In 1500, when London reached a population of 100,000, the next largest city in England was York at 20,000. As late as 1800, although London was the world's most populous city at 1,117,000, no other city in England had more than 100,000 people, and only about 12 percent of the population lived in cities.

The population of England shifted dramatically in the mid-1800s. The Industrial Revolution, a rapid change from an agricultural economy in which goods were largely hand crafted to one dominated by factory-based mass production and heavy industry, pulled people into the cities by the thousands. Liverpool grew from 82,000 in 1800 to 376,000 in 1850, Manchester from 75,000 to 338,000 over the same time period. In the mid-1990s, there were 89 cities of more than 100,000 population, led by London (6.9 million), Birmingham (1.1 million), and Leeds (721,000). Ninety-two percent of the English are categorized as city dwellers.

There has also been great growth in population overall. In the sixteen hundred years between 200 and 1800, England's population grew from 1 million to about 9 million. It then leaped to 32.6 million in 1900 and to nearly 50 million by 1996. This has resulted in a population density of about 974 people per square mile, higher than any other country except the Netherlands and Japan and ten times that of the United States.

THE "ENGLISH" PERSONALITY

The country's island setting has for centuries given its people the feeling that they stand apart from the rest of Europe. This has been reflected in the aloofness and reserve that seems so much a part of the English character. One observer commented dryly that the English have "all the qualities of a [fireplace] poker except for its occasional warmth."

Another factor contributing to the national character has been England's military history. Beginning with the Hundred Years' War against France in the Middle Ages and continuing through the defeat of Spain's mighty fleet in 1588, the period of empire building in the 1800s, and victories in World Wars I and II, the English developed a sense of superiority to foreigners. In the 1800s, the English applied the derogatory term "wogs" to nonwhites, and one Englishman went so far as to say haughtily, "The wogs begin at Calais [in France]."

Geography has also fostered another trait common to the English—an extraordinary politeness. The English are not usually inclined toward warmth and openness, but they treat one another and strangers with great civility. "Please," "sorry," and "thank you" are to be heard on busy London streets to an extent unthinkable in American cities. There is no pushing or shoving in lines for buses or for restaurant tables. To jump into a "queue," as the English call lines, is the height of rudeness. Social scientists have called this attitude a natural outgrowth of living on an island and having so many people in such a confined space, adding that the Japanese behave much the same way for much the same reason. The English, they say, have grown accustomed to using civility as a means of avoiding chaos.

Much as some alloys are stronger than any of their component metals, the English have drawn from many ethnic groups through the centuries to form a tough, resilient people. The second half of the twentieth century may have seen a decline in the fortunes of their country, but the English have a long history of overcoming defeat and adversity. Their tradition is one of the "stiff upper lip"—steadfastness in the face of calamity. Their resolve helped them become the mightiest nation on earth and may help them someday regain, at least in part, some of the prominence they have lost.

3

TOWARD A MODERN NATION

By 1800, England was the most powerful nation on earth, with an empire that circled the globe. Only about three hundred years earlier, however, she was a relatively unimportant island country on the edge of the civilized world—poor, militarily weak, far from the centers of politics and commerce. Furthermore, England in 1485 had just emerged from a bloody civil war. In a sixty-five-year period, six kings had come and gone, two of whom had been killed in battle and two others murdered. But a combination of geography and the energy of her people were soon to raise England to a position of power and respect.

The successful invasion by William the Conqueror brought England into closer contact with mainland Europe than ever before. Since William I was both king of England and a duke of France, he and many of his nobles held lands in both countries. By 1154, when Henry II became king, his dominions in France were actually larger than those of the king of France.

A FEUDAL SOCIETY

At this time, European society was based on a social, economic, and military system known as feudalism. Loyalty was sworn not to a country, but to one's overlord. A peasant owed allegiance to a knight, who owed allegiance to a baron, on up the social ladder to the king. Henry II, because of his lands in France, was a vassal of the king of France and was supposed to uphold the French king against all enemies. Such an arrangement proved unworkable, however, because the interests of France and England often came into conflict.

Henry's empire could not last: Neither Henry nor his successors could hold such a vast territory together amid shifting alliances and rivalries. By 1206, during the reign of Henry's son John—the Prince John of the Robin Hood leg-

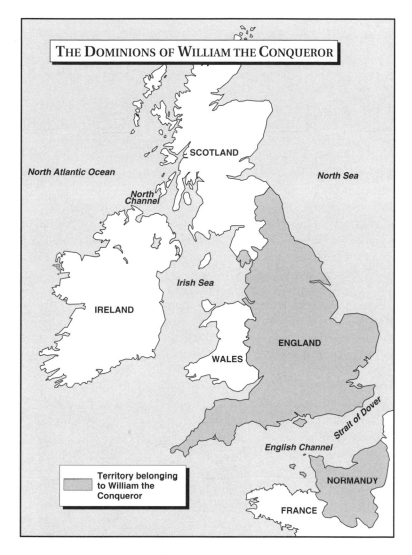

THE DOMINIONS OF WILLIAM THE CONQUEROR

North Atlantic Ocean

SCOTLAND

North Sea

North Channel

Irish Sea

IRELAND

ENGLAND

WALES

Strait of Dover

English Channel

Territory belonging to William the Conqueror

NORMANDY

FRANCE

ends—the kings of France had won back all the lands formerly held by England except a portion in the southwest known as Guienne. England had been a major power for the first time, but it had been so only because of its kings' connections to France.

THE HUNDRED YEARS' WAR

More than one hundred years later, a feudal conflict again led to war between France and England. Early in his reign, King Edward III of England had been forced to swear allegiance to the king of France for Guienne and the small

MURDER IN THE CATHEDRAL

One year after Henry II became king in 1153, he chose Thomas Becket to be his chancellor, or chief administrative official. Soon, Becket also became Henry's closest friend and adviser.

Henry's reign was marked by clashes with the church. One such difference was the issue of "criminous clerks." Under the law, a monk, deacon, priest, or anyone who had taken holy orders was tried for a crime in a church court rather than in the king's court. The church at this time contained many men and women of little education and loose morals. Some had entered the church to escape the law. Citizens complained that church courts often handed out slight punishments for major crimes.

In 1162, Henry saw a chance to change the law by appointing Becket to serve as archbishop of Canterbury, head of the church in England, as well as chancellor. Becket, extremely devout, warned Henry that he could not serve both the king and the church, but Henry would not listen. Then, to Henry's great surprise and dismay, Becket began to oppose him on the issue of criminous clerks.

In 1164, an assembly of nobles and churchmen produced the Constitutions of Clarendon, saying that a priest accused of a crime should be turned over to a king's court for punishment if found guilty by a church court. Becket, who had agreed to support the assembly's decision, changed his mind, resigned his office as chancellor, and fled to France for protection from Henry's wrath, remaining there six years before returning to Canterbury.

The quarrel culminated when Becket, with the pope's backing, excommunicated Henry, thereby cutting him off from the sacraments of the church. Henry, in a towering rage, shouted, "Such men I have about me. Will no one relieve me of this meddlesome priest?" Four knights took Henry at his word. They went to Canterbury Cathedral and, on December 29, 1170, murdered Becket before the horrified eyes of his monks.

The crime deeply shocked all Europe. Henry was forced to renounce the Constitutions of Clarendon and to submit to a humiliating apology. Becket's tomb quickly became a shrine, and he was canonized in 1173. In the end, however, Henry had his way. Becket's successor as archbishop agreed that priests accused of serious crimes should be tried by the king's courts.

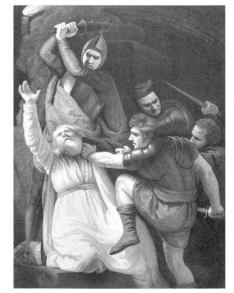

Thomas Becket pleads for his life as Henry's knights hack and stab him to death.

county of Ponthieu, which he had inherited through his mother, a princess of France. In 1337, Edward renounced his oath and claimed that he, through his mother, was the rightful king of France.

During the resulting struggle, known as the Hundred Years' War, England won some of the most famous battles in history: Edward III at Crécy, his son Edward the Black Prince at Poitiers, and Henry V at Agincourt. At one point, England again ruled most of France, and Henry V's infant son was crowned king in Paris. As with Henry II's empire, however, this vast area could not be held together. Inspired by a young peasant girl, Joan of Arc, the French rallied and by 1453 had pushed the English out of every part of France except for the port city of Calais.

French troops invade English-ruled Guienne in France during one of the battles of the Hundred Years' War.

A GROWING SPIRIT OF INDEPENDENCE

Two developments during the Hundred Years' War profoundly influenced a growing spirit of independence among the common people of England. The first was the Black Death, a plague that swept across Europe in waves starting in 1349 and killed about a third of the population. One result was a labor shortage, the first ever in Europe. The gulf between English peasants and their overlords was never as great as in other European countries. This gap shrank even more when ordinary farmworkers suddenly found themselves in great demand, with nobles competing for their skills. This brought about not only increased wages and a better standard of living, but also new feelings of self-worth and self-reliance.

The second development was a direct outgrowth of the war. The great victories were due not to the mounted knights on their warhorses, but to the English archers, common men whose arrows mowed down the French nobility like so much wheat. Until then, the ability to pay for a horse and armor made one a "gentleman" and put him on a plane high above the common soldier. The common soldiers' success in war brought them much closer in the social order to the knights. It is no accident that the victories at Crécy and Poitiers were followed later in the century by the Peasant's Revolt, during which the common people challenged the established class system. They used a rhyme to make their point:

When Adam delved and Eve span [spun cloth],
Where was then the gentleman?

A doctor visits a victim of the Black Death. The plague devastated Europe, killing a third of the population.

Although England actually lost territory as a result of the Hundred Years' War, the country benefited in several ways. First, the military reputation of the English was greatly enhanced. The contemporary chronicler John le Bel wrote that under Edward III the rest of Europe considered the English "the finest and most daring of warriors known to man." Second, the war cut England's centuries-old ties with France and made it a more unified nation. Third, and most important, the English language, which had been spoken primarily by peasants (Norman-French was the language of the upper classes), came into its own. French was rejected as the "enemy language." By 1385, according to one account of the time, "in all the gramere scoles of Engelond, children leveth Frensch and construeth and lerneth in Englische."

Edward I listens to his assemblies as he sits at the head of Parliament. Parliament's power grew during Edward's reign as he needed its support to collect taxes to fund the Hundred Years' War.

Another result of the long, expensive war was the growth in power of Parliament, England's legislative body. Parliament was a combination of two assemblies. One was the *magnum concillium*, or great council, which consisted of all the nobles in the kingdom, and on which kings relied to consent to taxation. The second, smaller group was called the *curia regis*, or king's court. The meetings of the *curia regis* were called the *curia regis in parliamento*, which eventually was shortened to Parliament after the French word meaning "to speak."

Edward I, who reigned from 1272 to 1307, began the practice of calling combined meetings of both groups as well as summoning knights and burgesses—non-nobles who represented towns or universities—from each shire. Parliament's power grew during the Hundred Years' War, mainly because kings needed its support to collect taxes to fight wars. Eventually, it was taken for granted that no tax could be levied without Parliament's consent.

The end of the Hundred Years' War brought no peace to England. Rather, a thirty-year civil war between rival branches of the royal family—the houses of Lancaster and York—broke out. The conflict was known as the Wars of the Roses for the flowers supposedly symbolizing the two sides, the red rose of Lancaster and the white rose of York. This was not a revolution or a war between classes. Instead, it was a largely internal struggle that divided the nobility on one side or the other. As a result, while large numbers of dukes, earls, and barons were killed and several ancient aristocratic families died out, cities prospered and the merchant class grew in power.

THE TUDORS

Another outcome of the Wars of the Roses was that, with the ranks of the nobility depleted and much of their power gone, the time was right for a strong monarchy to emerge. That was exactly what happened. The survivor of the war was Henry Tudor, a relatively obscure Welshman from a branch of the house of Lancaster. After the defeat and death of King Richard III, last of the Yorkists, at the Battle of Bosworth in 1485, he ascended the throne as King Henry VII, the first of a remarkably vigorous line of Tudor kings and queens.

Henry VII

Henry VII was just what England, worn out and impoverished by 150 years of warfare, needed. Cautious and frugal, he steered a careful diplomatic course between Spain and France—the two great European powers—encouraged trade, began English exploration in the New World, and, on his death in 1509, left England wealthy and at peace. He was succeeded by his son, Henry VIII, who was as extravagant as his father had been economical. He continued Henry VII's practice of ruthlessly putting down all opposition. Members of Parliament, fearful of being charged with treason or other crimes, did whatever the king wished.

Henry VIII is remembered chiefly for two things—his marital problems and removing England from the authority of the Roman Catholic Church. The two were related. Unable to persuade the pope, head of the church, to grant him an annulment from his first wife, the Spanish princess Catherine of Aragon, Henry had himself declared Protector and Only Supreme Head of the Church and Clergy of England. In the process, he confiscated the enormous wealth of the Catholic monasteries in England and used it to enrich himself and his supporters.

Henry VIII

Henry VIII was no religious reformer, as were Martin Luther and others of the time. He wanted a church with the same beliefs and the same trappings, only with himself instead of the pope as head. Others in England, however, wanted to reform the church. Despite Henry's wishes, England grew more and more Protestant, as those who broke from the Catholic Church were called.

The Protestant movement in England grew even stronger when Henry was succeeded in 1547 by his son, Edward VI. Edward was only nine years old when he became king, but he was highly intelligent and a fiercely devout Protestant. During his reign, the foundations of the modern Anglican Church were established. The English Prayer Book, written by Archbishop Thomas Cranmer, was published, and many of Henry VIII's laws restricting extreme Protestantism were repealed. Edward VI died of tuberculosis at the age of sixteen, however, and his half-sister, Mary, became queen.

Mary I

Mary I, daughter of Catherine of Aragon, was as ardent a Catholic as Edward had been a Protestant. In her five-year reign, she did everything in her power to return England to the Catholic faith. She married a Catholic prince, Philip of Spain, and dragged England into Spain's war with France. She brought Catholic priests and bishops back from exile. Finally, when many of her people refused to give up the Church of England, she had them burned at the stake. More than three hundred men and women, from bishops to shopkeepers, went to the flames. Mary's efforts were in vain, however. The executions intensified anti-Catholic

During her reign Elizabeth I helped end the internal religious conflicts that had plagued England for years.

feeling in England to the point that it became a permanent attitude. Mary died childless in 1588, and her half-sister, Elizabeth, took the throne.

THE REIGN OF ELIZABETH I

Elizabeth was, like her grandfather Henry VII, just the right person for the time. She was as cautious as he, and she had to be. She was only ten years old when her mother, Anne Boleyn, was executed. She herself was suspected several times of treason, against both Edward and Mary, and once was imprisoned in the Tower of London. These experiences taught her to trust no one completely, to keep her thoughts to herself, and to keep her emotions under control.

Elizabeth's immediate problem was that of religion. Her decision was typical for Elizabeth and perfectly suited to her country. What came to be called the Elizabethan Settlement resulted in a church that was moderate and surprisingly tolerant, something midway between the extreme views of her brother and sister. All church and government officials had to swear absolute loyalty to Elizabeth. Her title was Supreme Governor instead of Supreme Head of the Church. She had no wish to make herself the final authority on matters of faith: She was far more interested in political rather than spiritual control.

The Elizabethan Settlement was generally accepted by the people of England, most of whom simply wanted the religious strife to end and to be left to worship in peace. It was characteristic of the English that they were not as violent in their emotions as their European neighbors, about religion or anything else. The traditional English reserve was already in evidence, a tendency to keep one's thoughts private and to keep out of one's neighbor's business. Although all persons, by law, had to attend Church of England services, Catholics were allowed to practice their religion in private so long as they did not plot against the government.

Eventually, however, Catholics, encouraged by Spain and by the pope, did begin to plot against Elizabeth. When her throne was threatened, Elizabeth's spirit of toleration disappeared. Catholics were arrested, imprisoned, and heavily fined. Priests were imprisoned and executed. In 1587, Mary, Queen of Scots, Elizabeth's Catholic cousin, rival, and the person next in line for the crown, was executed after participating in a plot to assassinate Elizabeth.

War with Spain

Mary's execution brought to a climax discord with Spain that had been simmering for many years and was as much

The Six Wives of Henry VIII

One of the best-known figures in English history is King Henry VIII, not because of the justness or unjustness of his rule, but because of his matrimonial adventures. Many English kings married more than once, some three times, but Henry VIII far outdid all of them, taking six brides to the altar.

Henry's first wife, the Spanish princess Catherine of Aragon, had been married to Henry's older brother Arthur. When Arthur died, Catherine was engaged to Henry and they were married in 1509. Catherine was a loving, devoted wife and a great help to Henry, but she failed to bear a son. She also was six years older than Henry, whose roving eye soon settled on young, lively Anne Boleyn.

Henry tried to get his marriage to Catherine annulled, but the pope refused. As a result, Henry broke from the Catholic Church in 1534. When his new Church of England granted his divorce, he married Anne Boleyn.

Anne also failed to produce a son—only a daughter, the future Elizabeth I. Henry soon grew weary of her and found a new love, Jane Seymour. Anne was tried for adultery and, despite a lack of hard evidence, was found guilty and beheaded in 1536.

Henry immediately married Jane Seymour, who finally gave him the son he so desperately wanted but died in childbirth. The king remained unmarried for three years and then, for political reasons, agreed to marry a German countess, Anne of Cleves. When Anne arrived in England, however, Henry was repelled by her ugliness. He went through with the ceremony but quickly obtained a divorce.

His next marriage was for love, not politics. In 1540, at the age of forty-nine, he married beautiful, vivacious, twenty-year-old Catherine Howard. He was madly in love with Catherine, but she had married him only to become queen. She was secretly revolted by Henry and had several lovers. Henry was heartbroken when her adultery was discovered and she was beheaded in 1542.

A few years later, Henry married again. This time it was neither for love nor politics, but for comfort. By now, the king was a sick, bitter old man. His choice was a widow, Catherine Parr, who tended him in his illness until he died in 1547.

THE VIRGIN QUEEN

When Elizabeth I became queen of England in 1588, the most immediate question in the minds of her courtiers, other monarchs, and the pope was whom she would marry. England had had only one other reigning queen, Elizabeth's older half-sister, Mary, who had married Philip of Spain. It was taken for granted that Elizabeth would marry quickly. It was unthinkable that she would try to rule alone. For one thing, people reasoned, a woman could not possibly rule without a husband's help. For another, an heir to the throne would eventually be needed to prevent possible civil war.

Much might depend on Elizabeth's choice of a husband. Europe was divided between Catholics and Protestants, and Elizabeth's husband might make the difference in which direction England went. Spain and France, the two greatest powers in Europe, each feared she would marry someone from the other and form an alliance.

Elizabeth kept everyone guessing. She had suitor after suitor, starting with her dead sister's husband Philip, now king of Spain. She kept them all dangling, putting them off with pretty words and avoiding a decision.

Elizabeth probably only truly loved one man, Robert Dudley, her boyhood companion whom she made earl of Leicester. Leicester, however, already had a wife, and when she was found dead at the bottom of a staircase, people whispered that she had been murdered so that Leicester and Elizabeth might marry. Elizabeth realized that if she married Leicester she would lose the respect of her people and might lose her throne, as well.

Actually, she hated the very idea of marriage and probably from the first never intended to marry anyone. She had seen how marriage had turned out for her mother, the executed Anne Boleyn, and stepmother, the executed Catherine Howard. She also had no wish to share her power. "God's death!" she once shouted at Leicester. "I will have here but one mistress and no master."

Elizabeth never married, although the suitors and flirtations continued until she was well into her fifties. On her death in 1603, James VI of Scotland, son of Elizabeth's archrival Mary, Queen of Scots, became King James I of England.

economic as religious in nature. The discovery of the Americas in 1492 had dramatically altered the balance of power in Europe. Spain and Portugal had led the way in claiming and exploiting the New World. By 1578, when she absorbed Portugal, Spain, enriched by the silver mines of Mexico, threatened to dominate Europe.

The discovery of the Americas also brought about a dramatic change in England's position. Now, instead of being on the far fringe of affairs, which had centered around the Mediterranean Sea, she was in the center of the suddenly vital Atlantic trade. Because of Mary's alliance with Spain, however, England made few attempts to take part in this new source of wealth.

Elizabeth, however, was not willing to stand by and let Spain have a monopoly on trade with North America. English "sea dogs" such as John Hawkins and Francis Drake at one time had freely traded in Spanish ports in the Americas, but in 1568 King Philip of Spain forbade the practice. The result was an undeclared war with the English preying on Spanish shipping and Spanish ships ambushing English slave trade vessels.

Philip had been under pressure from the Catholic Church to invade England in order to remove Elizabeth from the throne and restore Catholicism. He had hesitated to do so, mostly because Elizabeth's successor would have been Mary, Queen of Scots, who, although a Catholic, had been brought up in France, Spain's enemy. With Mary dead, Philip decided to invade England. In May 1588 he sent the largest fleet the world had ever known, the Spanish Armada, to sail to the Spanish Netherlands to escort an invading army to England.

In a ten-day running battle up the English Channel to the coasts of France and the Netherlands, the English fleet, although outnumbered, managed to harass the Armada

The Spanish Armada retreats from the superior English fleet. After defeating the Armada, England enjoyed a reputation as a formidable world military power.

and eventually drive it away from its goal into the North Sea. Superior English seamanship, gunnery, and swift, nimble ships were able to defeat the lumbering, less maneuverable Spanish fleet.

The defeat of the Spanish Armada was a turning point in history, not only for England, but for the world. Had the invasion succeeded, Spain might have ruled all of Europe. The Protestant religion might have been crushed. Almost overnight, England became a respected military power for the first time since Agincourt. Her position in Europe was secure. Almost as important was what the victory did for the spirit of the English. There was a new sense of national pride, reflected in a great outpouring of literature, music, drama, exploration, and scientific discoveries known as the Elizabethan era.

THE RENAISSANCE IN ENGLAND

The Renaissance, a rebirth of classical culture that began in Italy about 1400, had reached England during the reign of Elizabeth's grandfather and took root under her flamboyant father. It was not English in character, however, but rather was a graft of Italian influences. The true English Renaissance began with Elizabeth, who loved literature, music, dancing, and whose dazzling court encouraged artists of all kinds. During and in the years just following Elizabeth's reign, Christopher Marlowe and William Shakespeare wrote their plays, Philip Sidney and Edmund Spenser wrote poetry, William Byrd developed the English madrigal, Francis Bacon laid the foundation for modern scientific inquiry, William Gilbert described for the first time the earth's magnetic field, and Walter Raleigh planted the first English colony in the New World on the shores of Virginia.

Despite many suitors and the constant pleas of her advisers, Elizabeth never married. When she died in 1603, the throne went to King James VI of Scotland, son of Mary, Queen of Scots. As James I of England, he was the first English ruler of the house of Stuart. Where Henry VII and Elizabeth had been exactly right for their times and places, James was exactly

William Shakespeare

wrong. He wanted to rule as absolutely as had Elizabeth, but had no feeling for the English people or England's Parliament. He made no attempt to earn the good will of his subjects, but instead insisted that he was "King by divine hereditary right" and that he was "God's lieutenant on earth." Whereas Elizabeth had persuaded members of Parliament to comply with her wishes for the good of the kingdom, James demanded they obey him blindly.

The story of the rule of James and of his son, Charles I, was one of constant struggle between the monarchy and Parliament. Parliament rejected the notion of a ruler with absolute powers, claiming that, although it had no right to rule, it had the right to lay down principles under which the king ruled. Both James and Charles tried to get along without Parliament, but both found themselves involved in foreign wars and needed Parliament to appropriate the necessary money.

Charles I

A growing influence during the reign of James were the Puritans—extreme Protestants who thought the Church of England too much like Catholicism and who believed in living as soberly and piously as possible. The fun-loving Elizabeth had hated the Puritans and had supported laws to force them to conform. After her death, however, the movement spread, particularly among middle-class merchants and well-to-do farmers.

CHARLES AGAINST PARLIAMENT

The Puritans were especially strong in Parliament, and when Charles I married a Catholic French princess, Parliament, in a protest vote, limited his import revenues to one year instead of for life, as was customary. Charles dismissed Parliament and tried to raise money by forcing wealthy subjects to lend it to him, clapping those who refused in prison. This violated the Magna Carta, a statement of rights that England's nobles had forced King John to sign in 1215. Charles, desperate for money to fight his wars, had to recall Parliament, which forced him to accept the Petition of Right, giving Parliament power to approve any tax or loan. Later, when Parliament began attacking the Church of England, Charles dismissed it again and had three members arrested.

Charles was able to rule without Parliament from 1629 to 1640, during which time the Puritans were so persecuted that many left England for the American colonies. Eventually, however, the king needed money to put down a rebellion by the Presbyterians of Scotland, whom he had tried to force to accept the Church of England. He called a Parliament that promptly arrested the king's two chief ministers and forced Charles to have one of them, the earl of Stafford, executed.

Parliament soon became divided on religious matters. Bills abolishing bishops and calling for reform of the church were passed, but only by a slim Puritan majority. The strength of the opposition led Charles to feel he had enough support to make a move. In January 1642 he led five hundred soldiers to Parliament, strode into the House of Commons, the chamber of Parliament for non-nobles, and demanded the arrest of five leaders. The leaders, however, had been warned and had escaped. Charles, frustrated and embarrassed, said, "The birds have flown," turned on his heel, and left. The king's attempt to bring Parliament to heel by military force made it impossible for the two sides to reconcile. War was inevitable.

London was strongly Puritan in its sympathies. When word spread of what Charles had done, the London militia declared its support of Parliament and vowed to protect its members from the king. A week later, Charles fled to northern England to try to organize support from the nobility there.

England's civil war had begun. It was a true war between classes over basic beliefs, not a simple clash for power as in the Wars of the Roses. Most of the Church of England clergy, the old nobility, and the large landowners stood with the king. Parliament was supported by the Puritans, the middle-class farmers and merchants, and the larger cities, particularly London. Those who followed Charles were called the Cavaliers; those who supported Parliament, Roundheads, because of their short haircuts.

THE TRIUMPH OF PARLIAMENT

Most of the trained soldiers and able commanders were on the king's side, and he held the advantage during the first two years of the war. Parliament, however, had greater financial resources with which to build up and pay an army. It also enlisted the help of Scotland with a promise to keep Scotland Presbyterian. Two Roundhead commanders, Oliver Cromwell and Thomas Fairfax, developed a professional and highly disciplined fighting force known as the New Model Army. Charles was defeated at Marston Moor in 1644 and at Naesby in 1645. After the latter battle, he surrendered to the Scots, who promptly turned him over to Parliament. When he sought to regain power, he was tried for treason against Parliament and was beheaded on January 30, 1649.

Once it had achieved victory, Parliament was too divided within itself to rule. Cromwell eventually expelled all Presbyterians from Parliament—called the Long Parliament because it sat from 1640 to 1648—leaving only sixty members,

Charles I receives a final comforting word from a clergyman before ascending the scaffold to his death.

Oliver Cromwell led a regime that suppressed the English people and left them longing for their old form of government.

known as the Rump Parliament. In 1653, Cromwell, backed by the army, expelled the rest of Parliament and ruled as a dictator with the title of Protector of the Commonwealth of England.

The Commonwealth was a grim, joyless land. Puritanism ruled. There was no dancing, no card playing, no theater, no music except for hymns. The vast majority of the English, moderate as always in their outlook and disliking extremism of any kind, soon wished they had the monarchy back. They were also tired of military rule and wanted the old form of government restored, only with more individual freedom than before.

When Cromwell died in 1658, his son, Richard, became protector but had none of his father's ability. Power fell into the hands of rival army generals, and the kingdom was on the verge of being torn apart. One of the generals, George Monk, realized the danger. He occupied London with his forces and called a Parliament that invited Charles's son, in exile in France, to return as king.

On May 23, 1660, King Charles II landed at Dover, and most of England rejoiced. England once again had a king, but this king had far less power and was far more dependent on Parliament. Although Charles and many of his successors tried to free themselves of parliamentary control, they had little success. The form of government that has endured to the present day had been established. It would enable England to achieve an empire such as the world had never seen.

THE RISE AND FALL OF EMPIRE

When Charles II became king in 1660, the bleak reign of the Puritans was over. The period known as the Restoration began. Theaters were reopened. Nobles entertained one another at lavish balls, and ordinary people danced in the streets. Underneath the gaiety, however, two important unresolved issues remained—government and religion. Only when they were settled would England rise to world prominence.

The Restoration was typically English. No blood was shed, except that Charles II insisted on the execution of a dozen men who had participated in the trial and execution of his father. Once again, the forces of moderation had triumphed. Just as England had revolted against kings who proclaimed they ruled by divine right, so she also had rebelled when the pendulum swung too far toward absolute state control. As usual, England sought a middle ground.

RELIGIOUS TENSION PERSISTS

The Restoration settled nothing in the area of religion. Most of the king's supporters wanted to force the entire country into the Church of England. A few favored religious liberty for all Protestants. No one wanted toleration for Catholics. The anti-Catholic feeling was especially important since both Charles and his brother James were strongly but secretly sympathetic to the Catholics, having been raised in France by their Catholic mother.

Charles tried his best to rule without Parliament, and almost succeeded. In need of money, he entered into the secret Treaty of Dover with the king of France, agreeing to help fight the Protestant Dutch and to restore Catholicism to England in exchange for cash. When he proclaimed toleration for Catholics, however, he had gone too far, and was forced by Parliament to accept the Test Act that required all officeholders to swear they were not Catholic or be

THE GREAT FIRE

On the night of Sunday, September 2, 1666, in London's Pudding Lane near the Thames River, a neglected coal from the oven of Thomas Farynor, the king's baker, set his bakery on fire. Four days later, most of the ancient city was a smoldering ruin.

The streets of London were narrow and tightly packed. Houses were built alongside one another and jutted out over the street so that people in upstairs windows across the street from one another could almost shake hands. The houses were all made of wood, the weather had been dry, and there was a strong east wind. It was a perfect recipe for disaster.

Whipped by the wind, the fire quickly spread to surrounding houses. Soon, much of the surrounding area was ablaze. People formed a line passing leather buckets filled with water up from the Thames River, but the dry wood went up like kindling. People abandoned the task and took to the river in any sort of boat they could find, taking what possessions they could save with them.

An observer and diarist, Samuel Pepys, wrote:

Everybody endeavouring to remove their goods, and flinging [them] into the River or bringing them into lighters [small boats] that lay off. Poor people staying in their houses as long as till the very fire touched them, and then running into boats or clambering from one pier by the waterside to another.

The fire eventually covered almost the entire city, burning throughout Monday and Tuesday before finally dying down on Wednesday. Then on Thursday, September 6, just when people began to return to what was left of their homes, the fire sprang up again on the west side of the city. This time, houses in the path of the fire were blown up with gunpowder and the blaze was contained.

Four-fifths of London had been destroyed, including most of the civic buildings, old St. Paul's Cathedral, eighty-seven parish churches, and about thirteen thousand houses. Some good, however, came from the disaster. When London was rebuilt, the job of designing many of the buildings, especially the churches, was undertaken by Christopher Wren. His new St. Paul's and fifty-one London churches remain some of the finest examples of English architecture.

dismissed. This did not apply to the king, but his brother, the heir to the throne, admitted to being a Catholic. Charles dissolved Parliament when it passed the Exclusion Bill barring James from the succession.

The country was again divided, and the division brought about the first political parties. Those who supported the king and his brother were called by their opponents Tories, a term referring to Irish bandits. The Tories retaliated by calling their foes Whigs, after a group of Scottish rebels. It was in Charles's reign that a king of England for the first time was forced to accept into his council a member of the party that held the majority in Parliament rather than being free to select his own ministers.

THE GLORIOUS REVOLUTION

James II succeeded his brother in 1685, but he had none of Charles's wit, charm, or cunning. After putting down a rebellion by Charles's illegitimate son, the duke of Monmouth, James proclaimed toleration for Catholics and admitted Catholics into the army and into universities. This was too much even for his Tory Parliament. They joined with the Whigs in inviting a Dutchman, Prince William of Orange, husband of James's older daughter, Mary, to come to England as king. James fled, and William and Mary shared the throne—the only time in English history husband and wife have ruled jointly.

William's bloodless invasion of 1688, called the Glorious Revolution, was yet another example of the English desire for peaceful, moderate solutions. And yet it indeed was a revolution. The Bill of Rights that year established

William and Mary accept the crown jointly, becoming the only husband and wife in the history of England to share the throne.

Parliament as an equal partner with the Crown and as the ultimate lawmaking body.

James, backed by the French, still posed a great danger to William. When James landed in Ireland with a French army and gained the support of the Catholic Irish, William led an army against him and defeated him at the Battle of the Boyne in 1690. Soon afterward, William introduced large numbers of Protestant settlers into northern Ireland, thus laying the groundwork for the religious warfare that continues in the late twentieth century.

With William defending his native Netherlands, France became England's enemy and would continue to be an enemy for most of the next two hundred years. Not much was settled during William's reign, but his wars led to an important political development. He found that the government ran far more smoothly when his ministers were all men of the same political party. Thus, the cabinet system was born.

After a few years of peace, war broke out again when the grandson of the king of France inherited the throne of Spain. England could not afford to see the Spanish empire fall into French hands. The ensuing War of the Spanish Succession (1701–1714) was another turning point in world history.

MARLBOROUGH'S VICTORIES

England's armies during the War of the Spanish Succession were led by John Churchill, duke of Marlborough, the greatest English general since Henry V. William had died in 1702, and, since Mary had already died childless, the throne had gone to her younger sister Anne. Marlborough's victories at Blenheim (1704), Ramillies (1706), and Oudenaarde (1708) broke the power of France. The Treaty of Utrecht in 1713 divided Spain's possessions.

The war and the treaty made England the world's greatest power. Throughout the 1600s she had established the thirteen American colonies along the Atlantic coast. In addition, English settlements were placed around Hudson Bay in Canada, and the East India Company was established in Madras, Calcutta, and Bombay. Through the Treaty of Utrecht, England added Gibraltar, Minorca, Nova Scotia, and Newfoundland to its growing empire.

Another addition, much closer to home, was Scotland. Ever since the death of Queen Elizabeth I, the kings and

queens of England had also ruled Scotland, but they were actually two countries with separate parliaments. The Act of Union in 1707 joined the two nations and the island became Great Britain. The flags of England and Scotland were joined to form the Union Jack, which remains Great Britain's banner today.

Only a few months after the end of the War of the Spanish Succession, Queen Anne died. None of her eleven children survived her, and the next in line for the throne was the exiled son of the late James II. He was a Catholic, however, so Parliament passed the Act of Settlement giving the crown to George, elector of the German principality of Hanover and a grandson of James I's daughter Elizabeth.

The duke of Marlborough's victory at Blenheim (pictured) helped end France's domination and solidified England's position as a world power.

GEORGE I

George I had little interest in England. He could not speak English, surrounded himself with cronies from Hanover, and generally left the governing of the country to his council. He did not wish even to preside over the council and left the task to the leader of the party in power. Although these terms were not yet in use, England now had a cabinet headed by a prime minister.

The next fifty years brought great internal peace and prosperity for England. Religious persecution was at an end, and even Catholics could worship openly, if not

THE QUEEN'S FAVORITE

Anne, the younger daughter of James II who became queen in 1702, was for much of her reign under the influence of one of her maids of honor, Sarah Jennings, who later became the wife of John Churchill, duke of Marlborough. Anne, lonely, not overly intelligent, and longing for a friend, encouraged Sarah to speak plainly to her. To remove the formalities, they pretended to be ordinary women in talking and writing to one another. Sarah took the name "Mrs. Freeman," and Anne was "Mrs. Morley."

Anne depended on Sarah for advice in all things, including politics. Sarah was a strong supporter of the Whig Party and used her influence with the queen to keep the party in power. She also used her place to further the military career of her husband.

When Churchill once threatened to resign from the army and, with Sarah, retire from public life, "Mrs. Morley" wrote this pleading letter to "Mrs. Freeman":

> The thoughts that both my dear Mrs. Freeman and Mr. Freeman have of retiring give me no small uneasiness and therefore I must say something on that subject. . . . Give me leave to say you should a little consider your faithful friends and poor country which must be ruined if ever you put your melancholy thoughts into execution. As for your poor unfortunate faithful Morley, she could not bear it; for if ever you forsake me I would have nothing to do with the world, but make another abdication; for what is a crown when the support of it is gone. I will never forsake your dear self, Mr. Freeman or Mr. Montgomery [Sidney Godolphin, the Lord Treasurer], but always be your constant and faithful friend, and we four must never part till Death mows us down with his impartial hand.

Eventually, Sarah took Anne's affection too much for granted and grew too domineering. Anne turned for friendship to another of her ladies, Abigail Hill, who steered her from the Whigs to the rival Tory Party.

Queen Anne

legally. The last threat from the house of Stuart came in 1745 when James II's grandson Charles, called "Bonnie Prince Charlie" by the Scots, mounted a revolt with French support. The Highlanders of Scotland supported him, but his army was routed at the Battle of Culloden Moor, the last major battle fought on the island of Britain.

Overseas, conflict with France continued. The two countries were vying with each other for colonies in North

America and India. The result was the Seven Years' War beginning in 1756 with England and the German state of Prussia allied against France and Austria. In addition to the fighting in Europe, the war was the first between European powers in North America, where it was known as the French and Indian War. At first, the war went badly for England, but under the direction of Prime Minister William Pitt the momentum shifted. Fort Duquesne was taken and renamed Pittsburgh. General James Wolfe captured the Canadian capital of Quebec. Robert Clive won great victories in India at Plassey and Madras. The war was ended by the Peace of Paris in 1763. England received all of Canada and control over much of India.

Suffering from a fatal bullet through his lungs, General James Wolfe is carried off the battlefield. The British victory at the Battle of Quebec settled the struggle between England and France for control over North America.

   Relations between England and her American colonists had been close during the fighting. That began to change when England demanded the Americans help pay the cost of the long war. The king, now George III, had abandoned the cabinet system for direct rule. Under his orders his chief

minister, the inept Lord North, pushed taxes and punitive measures aimed at the colonies through Parliament. When British troops tried to enforce them in 1775, fighting broke out in Massachusetts. The next year, on July 4, the colonies proclaimed their independence. With the help of France and other rivals of England, the Americans were eventually able to force the surrender of the main English army at Yorktown in 1781. The Treaty of Paris in 1783 ended English control over the colonies, which ultimately became the United States. The disaster ended the personal rule of George III. Parliament regained control of the government, and no English monarch since has attempted to direct the affairs of the country.

THE INDUSTRIAL REVOLUTION

The American Revolution had barely ended when England faced another revolution, one that did not involve armies and navies but would have effects more lasting than any military campaign. No one can say for certain when the Industrial Revolution began. Simple machinery had been taking the place of hand labor since 1700. Richard Arkwright's water-driven spinning machine of 1769, for instance, could

The British surrender their arms to General Washington in 1781. The American Revolution ended England's rule over the colonies.

THE FACE OF REVOLUTION

When poet William Blake called England a "green and pleasant land" in 1809 he probably did not realize how unpleasant some of it was already becoming. The Industrial Revolution had begun, and thousands of workers were moving from the countryside into factory towns. England was in the process of changing from a rural to an urban nation.

Cities such as Manchester and Birmingham doubled and tripled in size. Factories belched clouds of black smoke into the air. Soot coated the sides of buildings, killed trees, and filled every breath. Soon, the heavily industrialized area of northern England began to be called the "Black Land."

Charles Dickens painted an eloquent picture of a factory town, the fictional Coketown, in his novel *Hard Times*, written in 1854:

> It was a town of red brick, or of brick that would have been red if the smoke and ashes had allowed it; but as matters stood it was a town of unnatural red and black like the painted face of a savage. It was a town of machinery and tall chimneys, out of which interminable serpents of smoke trailed themselves for ever and ever, and never got uncoiled. It had a black canal in it, and a river that ran purple with ill-smelling dye, and vast piles of buildings full of windows where there was a rattling and a trembling all day long, and where the piston of the steam-engine worked monotonously up and down like the head of an elephant in a state of melancholy madness. It contained several large streets all very like one another, and many small streets still more like one another, inhabited by people equally like one another, who all went in and out at the same hours, with the same sound upon the same pavements, to do the same work, and to whom every day was the same as yesterday and tomorrow, and every year the counterpart of the last and the next.

do the work of twelve workers. It was a combination of events in the early 1780s, however, that transformed England and the world. First, in 1782, James Watt developed the steam engine. A year later Henry Cort developed a method of making iron using coal for fuel instead of wood. During this time, a system of canals was designed that would allow goods to be shipped far faster than over frequently muddy roads.

The iron to build machines and the engine to drive them led to the rapid development of mass-production industry, most of it located near the coalfields of the north. Within a few years, small towns such as Manchester and Birmingham became industrialized cities. Industrial production, combined with the wealth of the colonies, made England by far the wealthiest country in the world. Yet, the Industrial

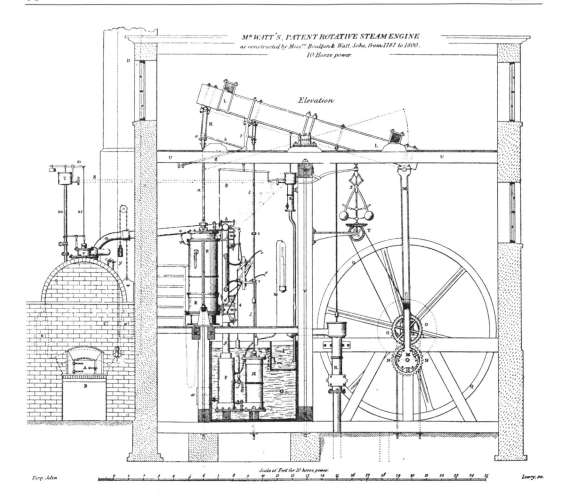

Mr WATT'S, PATENT ROTATIVE STEAM ENGINE
as constructed by Mess.rs Boulton & Watt, Soho, from 1787 to 1800.
10 Horse power.

Elevation

Scale of Feet for 10 horse power.

The plans for James Watt's steam engine. Watt's invention was one of the technological advances that fueled the Industrial Revolution in England.

Revolution had great social impact, as well. The spinners, weavers, and craftspeople of a thousand villages could not compete with the new factories and flocked to the cities to find work. The change from a rural to an urban society had begun. While the country was growing rich, an increasing number of meagerly paid workers lived in urban slums.

AN EXPANDING EMPIRE

Meanwhile, the empire continued to grow. In 1770 Captain James Cook discovered the continent of Australia. In 1788 an Australian colony was established at Botany Bay made up mostly of convicts. England would try to solve its growing problem of poverty and crime by "transporting" people to Australia in ever-increasing numbers.

Peace with France had never truly been achieved: The French Revolution in 1789 brought only a brief halt to hostilities. In 1793 the French, ruled no longer by a king but by Napoléon Bonaparte, invaded the Netherlands, defeating English troops there and touching off twenty years of warfare. Twice during the Napoléonic Wars England stood alone, all of her European allies conquered. Napoléon planned to invade England but was stopped in 1805 when the English navy commanded by Horatio Nelson defeated the French fleet at the Battle of Trafalgar.

During the war, England tried to blockade all ports trading with the French. This included American ports and led to the War of 1812 against the United States. Napoléon, however, had stretched his empire too thin. His army was driven out of Moscow in 1812 and destroyed by the harsh Russian winter as it retreated. Finally, in 1815, he was defeated at Waterloo. The subsequent Peace of Vienna gave England the Cape Colony at the southern tip of Africa, Ceylon, and Guiana.

Rebellion in the Air

Although England was now more wealthy than ever, more of her people were living in poverty as machines replaced hand labor. During and after the Napoléonic Wars, the Tory government took strict measures to secure the advantages of the ruling class. Trade unions were outlawed, and the Corn Law prohibiting the importation of cheap grain into England kept food prices high and put many families near starvation. Rebellion was in the air. Eight demonstrators were killed in Manchester in 1815. A plot was uncovered to murder the cabinet.

By 1820, even the Tories realized that reform was necessary. Trade unions were legalized. The harsh criminal code, under which stealing a pig could bring a death sentence, was overhauled. Catholics won the right to hold office. The reforms, however, split the Tory Party and the Whigs regained control of Parliament for the first time in sixty years.

Led by the prime minister, Lord Grey, the Whigs pushed for even greater reforms, including that of Parliament itself. At the time, members representing the various counties were elected, every man worth at least forty shillings having the right to vote. There were no guidelines, however, for choosing the representatives from the towns, or boroughs. Many times, great landowners nearby would simply handpick those who would support their interests. No change regarding borough representation had been made for centuries. A "rotten" borough, a town that had declined in population to a few dozen, might still send two members to Parliament while thriving cities like Birmingham were not represented at all.

THE GREAT REFORM BILL

The Whigs drew up the Reform Bill of 1832, which did away with the rotten boroughs and expanded the right to vote. The Tories vowed to defeat it, and the House of Lords voted it down. The House of Commons, however, forced the king, William IV, to promise to create enough new Whig nobles to give them a majority in the House of Lords. The House of Lords bowed to the threat, passed the bill, and the Reformed Parliament was elected in 1833.

Reforms now came more quickly. Slavery was outlawed everywhere in the British Empire in 1833. The Factory Act set strict limits on child labor in factories and mines. Cities above a certain size won the right of self-government. As important as these measures were, poverty was still widespread and only about 15 percent of adult men had the right to vote. Soon after Queen Victoria came to the throne in 1837, the working-class Chartist Movement presented a petition to Parliament demanding the vote for all men. It was rejected, and the Whigs lost favor with the people.

The new Conservative Party, built from the remnants of the old Tories, came to power in 1841. The prime minister was Robert Peel, who years before had instituted England's first police force, members of which were called "bobbies" after Peel. Peel believed in free trade and abolished many taxes on imported goods. Large landowners in the party, however, kept the hated Corn Law in place. At last, when failure of the potato crop brought famine to Ireland, Peel abolished the Corn Law in 1846.

The repeal of the Corn Law might have saved England from a bloody revolution of the kind that swept France and Germany in 1848. While the citizens of Paris fought troops from behind barricades and Germans rioted in the streets of Berlin, England was relatively calm. Once more, the English tendency toward moderation had prevented violence.

While Peel's action may have saved England, it tore the Conservatives apart. Those who favored free trade eventually combined with the Whigs to form the Liberal Party. The second half of the nineteenth century was marked by constant political shifts with first one party in power and then the other. It was a time of great prosperity and continuing reforms. The Reform Bill of 1867 gave the vote to small farmers and city workers. The Education Act gave control of schools to locally elected boards. The army was reorganized.

THE LABOUR PARTY

Still, the Conservatives and Liberals were the parties of the upper and middle classes. As trade union power began to grow, workers demanded even greater reforms. Several political societies were formed, including the Fabians, who favored armed revolution by the working class. Finally, under the leadership of Kier Hardie, the societies combined in 1900 to form the Labour Party.

Overseas, the empire continued to grow. In 1875 England bought the Suez Canal and began to control the affairs of Egypt. The island of Cyprus was taken from Turkey. Huge sections of Africa, including Kenya, Nigeria, Uganda, and Rhodesia, came under English rule. People began to say that the "sun never sets on the British empire."

But though England was still the mightiest nation on earth, potential rivals were getting stronger. The United States had emerged from the Civil War as an industrialized nation. Closer to home, Germany had finally become united after centuries as a collection of independent states. European powers began to outdo one another to build larger navies and grab more colonies.

The death of Queen Victoria in 1901 marked the high point of England's world power. The new century was marked early by increasing difficulties over Ireland. Ireland had become part of the United Kingdom in 1800 and had been sending representatives to Parliament. The Catholic majority in the southern part of Ireland, however, wanted "home rule," and many English politicians supported them. In 1911, with the House of Lords again forced to agree against its will, Ireland was granted its own parliament. Soon afterward, domestic peace was shattered by a series of violent strikes by miners and railway workers. The suffragette

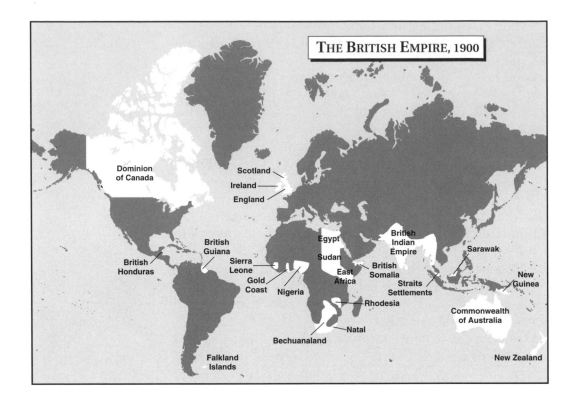

THE BRITISH EMPIRE, 1900

Dominion
of Canada

Scotland
Ireland
England

British
Guiana

British
Honduras

Egypt

Sudan

British
Indian
Empire

Sarawak

Sierra
Leone

Gold
Coast

Nigeria

East
Africa

British
Somalia

Straits
Settlements

New
Guinea

Rhodesia

Commonwealth
of Australia

Natal

Bechuanaland

Falkland
Islands

New Zealand

movement began demanding votes for women, and crowds of suffragettes battled police in the streets of England's cities.

A far greater conflict was on the horizon. Germany, a latecomer in the race for colonies, was growing increasingly aggressive. Her empire was growing, and she was rapidly becoming an economic rival of England. Finally, after a long series of crises, the bloody struggle known then as the Great War and now as World War I broke out. The war lasted four years, 1914 to 1918, after which England never recovered her former status. The cost, both in money and men, was staggering. The national debt was twelve times what it was before the war. A million men were killed or wounded.

BETWEEN WORLD WARS

Germany, only temporarily defeated, survived the harsh terms imposed by the Treaty of Versailles, survived the Great Depression of the 1930s, and—under the leadership of the National Socialist, or Nazi, Party and its fiery leader Adolf Hitler—rose up to challenge the world once more.

England, in comparison, appeared lost and without direction. Labor troubles persisted. The depression brought widespread unemployment. England's self-confidence seemed shaken. Instead of acting to stop Germany and Hitler, English politicians gave in to his every demand. At last, when Germany invaded Poland in 1939, England and France declared war on Germany and World War II began.

Germany quickly conquered Poland, then turned and made short work of France. Only an evacuation by hundreds of small boats prevented most of the English army from being trapped on the French coast at Dunkirk. England now stood alone, facing a threat of invasion greater than those posed by Philip of Spain or Napoléon. In 1940, with Hitler massing his forces for a crossing of the English Channel, the country was saved by a few hundred pilots who defeated the German air force in what became known as the Battle of Britain.

With the threat of invasion averted, England was able to hang on under the leadership of Prime Minister Winston Churchill until two events—the failure of the German invasion of the Soviet Union and the entry of the United States into the war—turned the tide. Victory finally came in 1945, but once again the price was high. The country was both exhausted and impoverished. Churchill was voted out of office and the first Labour Party government took over.

TWILIGHT OF EMPIRE

The British Empire was no more. Such nations as Canada, Australia, and New Zealand, which had been formally under the rule of the English Crown although they were largely self-governing, now were completely independent. One by one, the colonies broke free—India, Ceylon, Burma, Kenya, South Africa, Cyprus. Some stayed within an association known as the British Commonwealth of Nations. Others, such as Ireland, which had been granted its freedom while Protestant Northern Ireland remained part of Great Britain, chose to go their own way.

The country's economy was in a shambles after the war. The United States and the Soviet Union emerged as world superpowers. England, however, was slow to realize that her place had been so diminished. Other European countries could see that only through cooperation could they

King George VI inspects the bomb damage to London after a German air attack during the Battle of Britain.

hope to prosper. In the 1950s France and five other nations formed the European Economic Community, also called the Common Market. England continued its tradition of insularity. She refused to join and gradually fell behind as other nations' economies recovered. Not until 1973 did she finally join the EEC.

The economic troubles of England since World War II also changed the way in which the English viewed themselves. There have been brief moments of intense national pride, such as the coronation of Queen Elizabeth II in 1953 and the victory over Argentina in the Falklands War in 1982, but in general the attitude of the English has been one of discontent with the present and pessimism about the future. Pride in being English is present, but not to the extent it once was.

As the twenty-first century approaches, England faces a host of problems, some of them very familiar. Violence in Northern Ireland between Catholics and Protestants spills over into terrorism in England. Labor strife continues. Poverty has increased, especially among large numbers of immigrants from former colonies. Respect for law and tradition seems to be crumbling. Known for its civility, England is also known for the violence of its football fans. Even the royal family, at one time a revered symbol and the object of affection and respect, reels with scandal and divorce. England, once great almost beyond measure, faces a troubled and uncertain future.

ENGLAND TODAY

It is easy for Americans to think that because the countries share a common language and common traditions the differences between life in the United States and life in England are slight. There is a tendency to view England as "almost America," not as a foreign country whose language happens to be English. Americans seem to expect alien customs in France, Russia, or Japan, but not in England.

Certainly, there are many similarities. The same rock songs can be heard on radios in both London and Los Angeles. One can visit identical fast-food restaurants in York or in New York. Much of the similarity between the two countries, however, is superficial. In reality, many of the basic customs, lifestyles, and institutions of England are far different from those in the United States and very puzzling to visitors.

GOVERNMENT

England's legislative body, Parliament, has two houses, but members of only one, the House of Commons, are elected by the people. Seats in the House of Lords are hereditary or appointed, but this so-called upper house lost any real power decades ago and its role today is largely ceremonial. The House of Commons has 651 members, elected from districts in England, Wales, Scotland, and Northern Ireland.

The two primary political parties are Labour and Conservative. Although other parties, such as the Communist and Environmental, or Green, Parties exist, they have no seats in Parliament. On occasion, Parliament has had three parties, none of which held a majority of seats. In such instances, two parties have combined to gain a majority and form a coalition government.

The government is run by the cabinet, which is made up of the leaders of the party in power. Members of the cabinet head or have responsibilities in the various ministries, such as Defense, Education, Transportation, and many others. At the head of the cabinet is the prime minister, leader of the party in power.

General elections for the House of Commons are held at least every five years but may be held more frequently if the party feels it no longer has a working majority or if it thinks it can increase its majority. In such cases, the sovereign, on instructions from the prime minister, dissolves Parliament and calls for new elections.

A feature of English politics that Americans find strange is that members of Parliament need not live in the areas they represent. Instead, the party chooses which of its members will run in which districts. Party leaders and those who contribute the most money to the party run in "safe" districts, those that can be expected to easily elect the party's candidate.

Kings or queens have no direct political power. They have the right to be kept informed, to be consulted, and to make suggestions, but they cannot overturn any act of Parliament. Indeed, they are not supposed to even speak out on pending legislation or try to influence public opinion, although some have done so. Even the monarch's speech to open a session of Parliament is written by the party in power, and the king or queen is not permitted to change so much as a word.

Local government is in the hands of elected councils, which are responsible for providing such services as police protection and public housing. There are twenty-four such councils in Greater London alone. Local government used to be financed through a property tax, but since 1990 it has been funded by a poll tax, a fixed amount each person over eighteen must pay.

EDUCATION

English children begin their education by law at age five in primary schools, remaining there until they are eleven years old. Secondary schools are available for students ages eleven to nineteen, but students may leave school at sixteen. Unfortunately, about 65 percent do so.

Most English schools are financed through taxes and are free to students. About 6 percent of students, however, attend private schools—called public schools in England because their mission was to train people for public service. Private schools are very expensive, as much as $15,000 a year including fees and room and board. Many government schools have live-in students, as well, but room and board is not free.

The English school year is much longer than in the United States. School begins in early September and ends about the third week in July. English schools, however, have many more holidays. Almost all schoolchildren, girls and boys alike, wear uniforms. Uniform styles at some older private schools have not changed since the 1800s.

Individual schools formerly had a great deal of control over what was taught. The Education Act of 1988, however, created a so-called National Curriculum. Nine subjects—art, English, geography, history, mathematics, music, physical education, science, and technology/design—are taught in primary school. A tenth, foreign language, is added in secondary school. The compulsory teaching of foreign language was controversial, not surprising considering the traditional English aloofness toward the rest of Europe.

Formerly, all students were given an examination at age eleven to determine whether they would go on to a grammar school, which would prepare them for a university, or to a technical or trade school. This has been replaced by a series of exams in each subject. Students who pass the highest-level exams, given at age sixteen, receive a General Certificate of Secondary Education (GCSE) in that subject.

London children, dressed in traditional school uniforms, playfully pose for a photograph.

THE PLIGHT OF SCHOLARS

The first school at Oxford was begun sometime in the early 1100s. In 1167, English scholars, banned from the University of Paris as part of a quarrel between England and France, made their way to Oxford and by 1200 a university had been established.

For many years, Oxford University had no buildings. Lectures were given in churches or in rented halls. Eventually, individual colleges were endowed by wealthy benefactors and served not only as a place for lectures but also as dormitories and boardinghouses.

Students normally began their studies at about age fifteen, although there are records of Oxford students thirteen years old. They lived in crowded, often miserable conditions and, being high-spirited and rowdy, frequently fought in the streets with the citizens of the town.

Much like college students today, the scholars of Oxford tended to overspend their allowances and had to write home for more money. One surviving letter from a needy student to his father read,

I am studying at Oxford with the greatest degree of diligence, but the matter of money stands greatly in the way of my promotion, as it is now two months since I spent the last of what you sent me. The city is expensive and makes many demands. I have to rent lodgings, buy necessaries, and provide for many other things which I cannot now specify. There I respectfully beg your paternity that by the promptings of divine pity you may assist me so that I may be able to complete what I have well begun. For you must know that, without Ceres and Bacchus [the Greek goddess of food and god of wine], Apollo [the god of wisdom] grows cold. Farewell.

Those students who remain in school after age sixteen study for two additional years, at the end of which they may take A-level exams in the subjects they consider their strongest. Scores on A-level exams go a long way in determining which universities students may enter.

Higher education is not emphasized in England as much as in some other countries. Only 10.3 percent of people over twenty-five have some postsecondary education as compared with 21.2 percent in Germany, 26.7 percent in Japan, and 39.8 percent in the United States. All fees are paid by the government through grants averaging about $3,900 per year, and, depending on their financial circumstances, some students, receive grants for living expenses as well.

RELIGION

Religion has played a major role in English history. Wars have been fought and kings deposed in the name of religion. Today, however, religion is not of obvious importance to most of the people of England. Only about 8.4 million of Britain's 58.4 million people are active church members.

The Church of England remains the official religion of England. Elizabeth II, as queen, is the official head of the church. The church owns 18,700 church buildings, including everything from the grandest cathedrals to tiny village churches.

Despite being England's official church, the Church of England has only about 1.7 million members. Many of its largest buildings have congregations of only a few dozen worshipers. There are more Catholics in Great Britain than Anglicans, as Church of England members are called, and half as many Muslims.

The vast majority of the English seem indifferent to religion. Perhaps this is a result of centuries of religious strife. Perhaps the working classes are reacting against organized religion, which has often been viewed as the function of the aristocracy and the protector of the privileged. It may be a result, as some people claim, of widespread unemployment, urban decay, or a breakdown of family structure. Whatever the cause, says one prominent scholar, "People are suspicious of church practices and the hide-bound philosophies therein. They find it difficult to relate Christianity to their daily life."

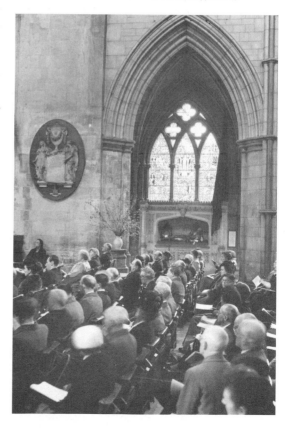

Though religion has figured prominently in English history, only a small percentage of today's English population attends church regularly.

THE WELFARE STATE

In the 1800s, when the British Empire was at its zenith, the upper classes grew wealthy while masses of agricultural and factory workers lived in grim poverty. Public services were almost nonexistent. Able-bodied but unemployed persons were forced into bleak "workhouses" of the type deplored by Charles Dickens in his novels. Once their working days had ended, the elderly were largely on their own.

Since 1900, however, the situation has almost completely reversed. Decades of social reform, most of it enacted when the Labour Party was in power, has placed heavy taxes on the wealthy and established a "cradle to grave" system of services. Poverty still exists, but all English citizens are guaranteed health care, housing, a subsistence income, and old age pensions.

Health care is provided by the National Health Service, established in 1948. Free health care is provided to everyone in England, even tourists. The only charges are for dental work, eyeglasses, and prescription medicine, although these are free to children, the elderly, and the poor. Individuals are free to choose their own doctors and to change doctors whenever they wish. Doctors admit their patients to government-owned hospitals.

HEALTH CARE DRAWBACKS

The drawbacks to the National Health Service are that doctor visits frequently entail long waits and exams are too often brief and cursory. Hospital facilities are limited, especially those equipped for surgery. People needing non-emergency surgery must frequently wait for months.

Many of the English who can afford it have private doctors and go to private hospitals where immediate care is available. Those who do so usually have private medical insurance, which is extremely expensive. Many doctors who are paid a salary by the government supplement their income through private practice and have been accused of giving greater attention to their paying patients.

On the whole, however, the National Health Service seems to do a good job of providing basic health care at a reasonable cost to the country. England spends about 6 percent of gross income on health care compared to about 12 percent in the United States.

In addition to health care, free or subsidized housing is provided to the poor by local government councils. Just as with public housing in the United States, however, there are long lists for these "council houses."

Every employed person in England and all employers pay into the National Insurance Fund, which in turn makes cash payments to the unemployed who lose their jobs through no fault of their own or who are injured on the job and cannot work. The National Insurance Fund also provides retirement benefits for those who have paid into it. Men are eligible to receive pensions at age sixty-five and women at sixty. These pensions, while by no means lavish, provide more financial support than does the U.S. system of Social Security.

Those who do not pay into the National Insurance Fund are eligible to receive cash payments, sometimes called the dole, if their income is below certain levels. These funds come from general tax revenues, as do payments to poor children, usually paid to the mother.

THE ECONOMY

The Industrial Revolution made England the wealthiest country in the world in the 1800s. Two major wars and a severe economic depression in the 1900s left her behind many of her European neighbors. The 1980s and 1990s, however, witnessed a growth in business activity that has placed England once more among the major economic powers.

Three major events in the 1970s contributed to the resurgence of the English economy. First, large deposits of oil were discovered under the North Sea. As a result, the oil industry is one of the country's largest employers, and England has become an exporter of oil instead of being dependent on imports. Second, the country was admitted to the European Economic Community in 1973 after years of first refusing to join then being kept out by France's veto. Since then, trade with European neighbors has improved dramatically, although the United States remains England's single largest trading partner. The third event was the return to power in 1979 of the Conservative Party under Prime Minister Margaret Thatcher. The Conservatives' policies of encouraging more investment in industry and removing legal restrictions on business led to increased economic growth.

Oil deposits in the North Sea greatly contribute to England's economy.

Part of England's economic turnaround has been a movement away from the nationalization of industries. In the decades after the Labour Party gained power in 1945, the government took over such industries as coal, iron and steel, airline service, electric power, and telephone service. In the Thatcher government, which lasted until 1990, many of the more profitable nationalized industries were sold to private companies. As a result, English investors, who had been going increasingly overseas, began to look closer to home to spend their money.

Most employment in England is in the service industries. Businesses such as retail stores, advertising, computer systems, marketing, and leisure-related services such as hotels and the travel industry are now employing about 68 percent of the English workforce. Manufacturing employs about 29 percent compared to 34 percent in 1982 and 50 percent before 1900. Although England exports high-quality electronics equipment, computers, and aerospace equipment, much heavy machinery that used to be manufactured in England is now imported from countries where labor is less expensive. Only 2 percent of the population was employed in agriculture in the 1990s, down from 21 percent in 1851. Mechanized farming, however, has kept crop yields high, and England has to import only about one-tenth of her food supply.

England's standard of living is among the world's highest. The literacy rate is nearly 100 percent. Sixty-eight percent of all households have private automobiles, a high figure considering the number of large cities in which private autos are the exception. Ninety-nine percent have refrigerators; 98 percent, televisions; and 70 percent, videocassette recorders. Despite the density of the population, only eight nations have more average rooms per household. The average life expectancy is 75 years as compared to the worldwide average of 63.3.

The economic well-being of the English over the years has generally increased with the population. Although there was still a

Under Prime Minister Margaret Thatcher, England regained its position as an economically viable country.

sharp division between the rich and poor after the Industrial Revolution, the general standard of living rose and continued to grow well into this century, except for a distinct drop during the Great Depression of the 1930s. World War II, however, almost bankrupted England. Before 1940, it was the world's leading economic power. After 1945, rationing of food and fuel continued for almost ten years, unemployment was high, and there was great labor unrest. The country suffered from waiting so long to join the European Economic Community. Although the economy began to improve dramatically in the late 1980s, Great Britain ranked only seventeenth in the world in 1994 in per capita gross national product (the total worth of goods and services produced).

Although England's standard of living is high compared with that of the rest of the world, it lags behind most of the other industrialized nations. The per capita income (in U.S. dollars) was $16,070 in 1995 compared with $17,080 in Australia, $18,690 in the United States, $19,480 in France, $25,430 in Japan, and $32,790 in Switzerland. Unemployment has been higher than for other EEC countries. Unemployment in Great Britain rose from 5 percent in 1979 to 10.4 percent in 1993, then fell to 8.3 percent in 1995, more than 2 percent higher than in the United States.

LEISURE ACTIVITIES

Leisure time has always been extremely important to the English, who have originated several ways to spend it. Getting away for the weekend was essentially an English innovation. Rugby football, association football (soccer), and cricket all began in England and draw huge numbers both as spectators and participants. When they stay at home, the men and women of England can often be found in their gardens.

The English are great travelers but seldom world travelers. Perhaps because the English have traditionally been wary of foreign places, far fewer of them go overseas than do their European or American counterparts. Those who can afford foreign travel seldom go farther than warm, sunny Spain.

Travel within Britain, however, is enjoyed by almost everyone. During the summer months, roads and highways are clogged with people heading to the beach, where there is more sunbathing than swimming thanks to the chilliness

Playing Rough

The sport of association football, known in the United States as soccer, supposedly got its start in England when Anglo-Saxon farmworkers plowing a field unearthed the skull of a Danish warrior killed in battle a few years earlier. To show their still-bitter feelings for the Danes and also to amuse themselves, the workers began kicking the skull among them. This early form of football was called "kicking the Dane's head."

In due time, a ball was substituted for the skull and football began to gain in popularity. Sometimes games matched all the men of one village against those of a neighboring village, the object being to kick the ball onto the other's village green, the entire distance between the villages being the "field."

There were no rules, and the games were incredibly rough. In 1583, a disapproving Philip Stubbes wrote:

> Doth not everyone lie in wait for his adversary, seeking to overthrow him and to pitch him on the nose, though it be upon hard stones, in ditch or dale, in valley or hill, or what place soever it be, he careth not, so he have him down? And he that can serve the most of this fashion, he is counted the only fellow . . . so that by this means sometimes their necks are broken, sometimes their backs, sometimes their legs, sometimes their arms; sometime one part thrust out of joint, sometime another; sometime the noses gush out with blood, sometime their eyes start out.

Only part of Stubbes's objection was the roughness of the game. He and his fellow clergymen also deplored football because it was played on Sundays. The government also took a dim view of football, thinking time could be better spent practicing archery. Several laws were passed banning football, but none was successful.

An 1875 engraving depicts the time-honored game of English football.

of the water. Others take to the mountains or the moors, where camping and hiking are very popular. Bicycling is also widespread, and members of cycling clubs often go on weekend cross-country trips.

Team sports are tremendously popular. Professional soccer is the top spectator sport, drawing millions of fans each year. Indeed, English soccer fans have grown so enthusiastic and rowdy that some other countries have banned them from international matches. Rugby, a game more like American football, is also popular, as is the ball-and-bat game of cricket, although the latter is considered more of a "gentleman's game." All three team sports are played in most English schools.

The most prevalent individual sports are golf—invented in neighboring Scotland—tennis, and track and field. The British Open is one of golf's four major championships, and the British National Tournament at Wimbledon is the most prestigious tennis championship in the world. Track is far more popular than in the United States. Many cities and towns have amateur track clubs that compete against one another.

Horse racing is probably more popular in England than in any country on earth. Kings and queens from James I to Elizabeth II have owned and raced thoroughbreds, and the annual race meeting at Ascot is one of the premier social events in England. The most important race is the Derby, run annually since 1780 and the namesake of many other races, such as America's Kentucky Derby. Racetracks are far more common than in the United States and can be found in most large and medium-size cities.

English players team up to tackle a South Wales opponent during a competitive game of rugby.

Gambling on sports events is almost as popular in England as attending them. Betting is legal throughout the country, and almost every town has a licensed "betting shop." The English love to "take a flutter," as wagering is called, and people from all walks of life will bet on anything from a local soccer match to a foreign presidential election.

No account of leisure activities would be complete without mentioning that most English of institutions, the public house, or pub. The earliest public houses were the inns and taverns of the Middle Ages, which provided food, drink, and shelter to travelers for a price. The term "pub" has today come to mean an establishment in which alcoholic beverages are sold.

Since the English are among the leading per capita consumers of alcoholic drinks, it is understandable that there are thousands of pubs. The smallest villages have at least one pub, and one seems to anchor every street intersection in the business districts of cities. They serve not only as a place for drinking, and sometimes eating, but as places for neighbors to meet and exchange news or gossip. Most pubs were formerly all-male establishments with perhaps a side room where women were welcome. The all-male pub is now found only in remote rural areas.

Horse racing is a popular sport in England, especially among England's royalty.

A BEER-LOVING COUNTRY

The English have long had reputations as heavy drinkers of alcoholic beverages. As early as 1285, an Italian visitor wrote, "The English delight in drink and make it their business to drain full goblets." But, whereas wine was the universal drink in Italy and France, beer was the favorite in England.

The Anglo-Saxons brewed and drank beer and ale in great quantities. A favorite drink was mead, ale mixed with honey. A record of taxes on beer in the late 1600s indicates that the average consumption at that time was three quarts per person per week.

To some foreigners, it seemed as if the English (except for the nobility, who preferred wine) drank nothing *but* beer. A Frenchman, César de Saussure, wrote in the 1700s:

> Would you believe it, though water is to be had in abundance in London and of fairly good quality, absolutely none is drunk? The lower classes, even the paupers, do not know what it is to quench their thirst with water. In this country, nothing but beer is drunk, and it is made in several qualities. Small beer is what everyone drinks when thirsty; it is used even in the best houses and costs only a penny the pot. Another kind of beer is called porter, meaning carrier, because the greater quantity of this beer is consumed by the working classes. It is a thick and strong beverage, and the effect it produces, if drunk in excess, is the same as that of wine; this porter costs threepence the pot. In London there are a number of alehouses, where nothing but this sort of beer is sold. There are again other clear beers, called ale, some of these being as transparent as fine old wine, foreigners often mistaking them at first sight for the latter. . . . It is said that more grain is consumed in England for making beer than for making bread.

THE ENGLISH THEATER

The English love affair with the theater goes back hundreds of years to a time when monks performed "mystery" plays to present biblical stories to their illiterate congregations. Later, wandering troupes of actors brought plays to towns and villages. Drama flourished during the reigns of Elizabeth I and James I, when Londoners flocked to the plays of William Shakespeare and Christopher Marlowe.

As a result of this rich tradition, the English are among the most devoted playgoers, and London can rightfully claim to be the theater capital of the world. Some of the most famous theaters in history, such as the Savoy and the Theater Royal in Drury Lane, abound in the West End section, where all the latest hits and most spectacular musicals can be seen. Audiences include college students who buy inexpensive seats high in the balcony and wealthy patrons who may pay the equivalent of two hundred dollars for a seat.

The West End, however, is merely the starting point for one who wishes to explore the London theater scene. The National Theater on the south bank of the Thames River is famous for its production of Shakespeare's plays. Theaters in the Sloane Square area present new works by lesser-known playwrights, and thousands come to the outdoor theater in Regent's Park in the summer.

English theater extends far beyond London. There are many exceptional theatrical companies in such cities as Manchester and Leicester, and the Royal Shakespeare Company at Stratford-upon-Avon is considered the finest in the world at bringing Shakespeare's works to stage. Several cities also have periodic theater festivals. One of the most outstanding has been at Chichester, which over the years has featured such performers as Laurence Olivier, Alec Guinness, Ben Kingsley, and Maggie Smith.

LANGUAGE

Although England is a small country, it has an amazing variety of language and customs. It is sometimes difficult for the Liverpool dockworker, the East London cab driver, and the Plymouth fisherman to understand one another, let alone be understood by American visitors. For centuries, most people lived and died within a few miles of their birthplace. Even now, there is far less mobility among the English than among other peoples. This has led to a wide diversity in everything from food to fashion.

Most people in England speak a dialect far different from the formal, dignified language spoken by the royal family. "Know what I mean?" will become "Knoaw wot oi maen?" in the mouth of the Cockney, a person born within the sound of the bells of St. Mary-le-Bow in East London. The Yorkshire farmer will say "summat fra nowt" instead of "something from nothing." And "I'm sorry, sir" will come out "Izzorry, zir" in the soft buzz of Devonshire. In this century, however, with "standard" English heard throughout the country on radio and television, regional speech patterns have become less prevalent.

Another stumbling block for visitors is the bewildering number of slang terms that have a totally different meaning in England. A "nick" is not only a small cut but also a verb meaning "to steal" and another name for a jail. "Knickers" in England refers not to old-fashioned boys' trousers but to underpants. Even more mystifying is the rhyming slang of the Cockneys in which "telephone" becomes "dog and bone" and "wife" is "trouble and strife."

POPULAR CULTURE

Before the 1960s, the popular view of the English throughout the rest of the world was that they were drab and stuffy. England was the last place one might expect to become a global leader in music and fashion, yet that is what happened.

Because of the extent of the British Empire, England had long set the style in men's clothing. The finest, if also the most conservative, suits came from Saville Row and Bond Street in London. France was the leader in women's fashions. In the mid-1960s, however, the fashion center of the world was London's Carnaby Street, and it was anything but conservative. The sixties look—miniskirts and bell-bottomed trousers—began in London and quickly spread worldwide. Ever since, London has been a leader in fashion, particularly in trendy clothing for young people.

England has become well known for its musical theater. Many successful musicals, such as Cats *and* The Phantom of the Opera, *originated in England.*

The Beatles, perhaps the most famous music group of all time, revolutionized popular music in the 1960s.

Going hand-in-hand with the revolution in clothing was the revolution in music. England had been famous for her madrigals and church music during the reign of Elizabeth I, but not much of her music was popular outside the country since then. One exception was the operettas of Sir William Gilbert and Sir Arthur Sullivan. The breakthrough in popular music came when the Beatles, Rolling Stones, and other groups, all influenced by American jazz and rock music, took the world by storm in the 1960s. England once again became the leader in show music in the 1970s and 1980s when such Andrew Lloyd Webber shows as *Jesus Christ Superstar, Cats,* and *The Phantom of the Opera* became smash hits.

One consequence of England's influence on popular culture has been to redefine the country's image. Instead of the proper businessman or the highborn lady at afternoon tea, the picture that may come to mind is that of the punk rocker with spiky, multicolored hair. It is not an image with which the older generation in England is comfortable, but it reveals much about how much the country has changed and departed from tradition in the last decades of the twentieth century.

The Land Where History Lives

England is a modern nation. The skyscrapers of its cities house multinational corporations and are topped with satellite dishes. Her high-tech products are marketed worldwide. Commuters are whisked to work in clean, efficient subways or on modern superhighways. All the trappings of the 1990s—cellular phones, fax modems, pagers—abound.

And yet, one is never far away from historical England. The modern town sits in the shadow of a castle built almost a thousand years ago. A cottager digging in his garden turns up a bagful of Roman coins, buried in haste by someone fleeing a barbarian invasion. Villagers attend church in the same stone buildings in which their ancestors have worshiped since before Columbus.

Indeed, it is almost impossible to escape the atmosphere of history that seems to linger over the entire country. Even in the most industrial cities, castles and cathedrals are right around the corner from railway stations and office buildings. Stately mansions dot the countryside. Even the exit signs from the motorways speak the names of history—Stratford-upon-Avon, Canterbury, Nottingham, Runnymede.

Preservation of Heritage

To some extent, the emphasis on historical England is no accident. England is one of the top tourist destinations in the world. Citizens of the dozens of countries once under British rule flock to the country from which their own traditions sprang. The English recognize the economic importance of what they call the "heritage business" and have taken care to preserve that heritage.

Preservation of historical places in England, however, is much more than good business. It is in keeping with the English reverence for tradition. The "beefeaters" who patrol the Tower of London wear the same uniforms as in the days of Elizabeth I. Judges wear the same horsehair wigs as in

England gracefully integrates its heritage with the present. (Above) A modern beefeater, wearing a traditional uniform, stands guard at the Tower of London. (Right) A skyscraper looms behind a historical London church.

the 1700s. Even if most English would agree that a certain custom or practice is no longer useful and, indeed, may be impractical, far fewer are willing to change it.

Thus it is that the English, who take great pride in their past, have taken care to ensure that it has its place among the new and the modern. It is impossible to understand present-day England without experiencing the past. Fortunately, that past is to be found almost everywhere, from major tourist attractions thronged each day with thousands to quiet, out-of-the-way places that visitors may see and touch in privacy, taking themselves back hundreds, even thousands, of years.

ANCIENT ENGLAND: STONEHENGE

Each day, buses unload hundreds of tourists onto the grassy plains of Wiltshire about ten miles north of Salisbury

at a circle of stones, many of them now broken and tumbled down. The site is known as Stonehenge, but exactly who built it, when it was built, and why it was built remain uncertain.

Stonehenge was already ancient when the Romans arrived. Experts think, but are not sure, that it was begun about 2200 B.C. and finished some nine hundred years later. At the core of the complex was a circle of huge sandstone blocks, topped by lintels. Inside the circle was a horseshoe of seven pairs of huge upright stones of forty-five tons, also capped with lintels.

The builders of Stonehenge had to bring the enormous stones from as far away as southern Wales, 240 miles distant, but no one knows how this was accomplished. Some think the stones were floated around the coastline and up rivers using huge rafts.

No one knows why Stonehenge was built or how it was used. The stones are positioned so that one looks through the main gateway down the avenue leading to the circle to the exact point at which the sun rises on Midsummer Day. This suggests that Stonehenge may have been used for sun worship, but there is no proof. Some have imagined that Stonehenge was used by the Druids for human sacrifice.

Experts believe that the mysterious stone circles at Stonehenge date back to 2200 B.C. The site has been a popular tourist attraction since Roman times.

Archaeologists estimate that the stones at Avebury (pictured) were erected at about the same time as those at Stonehenge. The purpose of the stone monuments continues to baffle experts.

The Druids, however, were priests of the Celts, who did not come to Britain until much later.

As late as the 1970s, visitors were allowed to walk among and touch the stones. Vandalism and souvenir hunting, however, resulted in the erection of a wire fence, thereby spoiling the visit for those who want to experience closely something so ancient.

ANCIENT ENGLAND: AVEBURY

For every thousand people who visit Stonehenge, perhaps only a dozen will travel twenty miles farther north to Avebury. Though Stonehenge was a tourist attraction in Roman times, Avebury drew little attention until a book describing it was published in 1743.

Like Stonehenge, Avebury is a circle, but a much larger one. The diameter is about fourteen hundred feet, and most of the village of Avebury lies within its circumference. Just inside the circular earthworks was a ring of about one hundred large, upright stones, twenty-three of which still stand. Two additional circles, each about thirty feet across, were inside the large circle.

From the large circle a road lined with large stones extended more than a mile southeast to where archaeologists have found ruins of a building they call the Sanctuary. Although the stones of Avebury appear more crude and unfinished than those at Stonehenge, the structures are thought to have been built at about the same time.

Avebury probably had some religious significance, but that is only a guess. No connection of the stones with the positions of the sun, moon, or stars has ever been discovered.

Unlike Stonehenge, Avebury can be experienced firsthand. It is a short walk from the parking lot into the southwest quadrant of the large circle. Visitors can wander among the stones, taking care to watch where they step since the field is used to graze sheep. A grove of trees atop the thirty-foot-high earthworks provides a good spot to rest, enjoy a picnic lunch, and reflect on the monument and the people who built it.

ROMAN ENGLAND: BATH

In the early 1100s, Norman nobles noticed hot water bubbling up from the ground at a site about 110 miles west of London. They built an enclosed pool at the site for relaxing

THE NATIONAL TRUST

In the 1800s, many of the most famous places in England—from Roman ruins to fabulous country homes—were in danger of being lost. In some cases, such as at Hadrian's Wall, local farmers were taking stones to use to build walls around their fields. In other cases, aristocratic families found centuries-old homes uncomfortable and virtually abandoned them for life in the city.

In the 1860s, a woman named Octavia Hill established the Open Space Movement, the goal of which was to preserve open spaces within cities and to tear down slums and replace them with mass housing bordered by parks. Using money lent to her by artist and writer John Ruskin, she established the first modern housing project in the St. Marylebone area of London in 1864.

Hill later became interested in preserving buildings of historic interest and making them accessible to the public. Along with Sir Robert Hunter and the Rev. Hardwicke Rawnsley, she established the National Trust for Places of Historic Interest or Natural Beauty in 1895. In 1907, Parliament passed the National Trust Act giving the organization wide powers to act to save historic sites.

The National Trust's first property was an area of parkland overlooking Cardigan Bay in Wales. Today, the Trust owns almost 700,000 acres and about 350 homes, castles, gardens, and other places of interest, including Hadrian's Wall, Runnymede (where the Magna Carta was signed), and Sir Winston Churchill's home at Chartwell. In some cases, families wishing to avoid heavy property or inheritance taxes have turned their homes over to the National Trust with the provision that they and their heirs can continue to live there.

in the 120-degree mineral waters. The place was called King's Bath, later shortened to Bath. In the 1700s Bath became a fashionable place for members of London society, even royalty.

In 1878, however, workmen excavating a site in the center of the city discovered that the Normans were by no means the first to turn the hot water to their own use. They found the remnants of baths built a thousand years before the Normans by the Romans, who had named the site *aquae sulis* (water of the sun) and built a temple nearby dedicated to the goddess Minerva.

Tourists today can walk among ancient Roman baths in England. Though the baths are no longer in use, hot water still flows through the baths' lead pipes.

Descending some twenty feet below the level of a busy, downtown street, visitors can walk through this series of ancient baths and pools reminiscent of today's health club. The Great Bath was used for swimming, and there were a number of smaller baths in which people sat as in modern

hot tubs. There was even a room filled with steam from hot water circulated under the floor, like a sauna. After soaking in the hot water, the Roman bather could take a refreshing plunge in a nearby pool of cold water.

Remnants of Hadrian's Wall, originally built in A.D. 123, still stand today.

It would be possible, though not allowed, to bathe as the Romans did almost two thousand years ago. Hot water still flows through the original lead pipes and channels into the Great Bath, which is still waterproofed with the original sheets of lead. Visitors walk on Roman paving stones while, from the railing overhead, come the sounds of motorcycles and taxis.

ROMAN ENGLAND: HADRIAN'S WALL

Unlike Bath, Hadrian's Wall is not on most tourists' must-see list. The primary reason is that it is harder to reach, off the major highways and about three hundred miles north of London.

In A.D. 123, Hadrian, emperor of Rome, declared that Scotland was not worth the trouble it would take to conquer it. He ordered a wall built from the Tyne River near the east coast to the Solway Firth in the west, a distance of seventy-three miles. It was intended to keep Roman Britain safe from raids by the wild tribes to the north.

Westminster Abbey, one of England's oldest and most famous churches, contains the tombs of hundreds of famous subjects and English monarchs.

For most of its length, Hadrian's Wall was fifteen feet high and ten feet wide. There were towers every third of a mile and a fortified gate called a "milecastle" every mile. Each milecastle was manned by about twenty legionnaires. They were supplied and reinforced from a series of forts, the largest of which could house up to one thousand soldiers. On the north side of the wall the Romans dug a ditch ten feet deep and thirty feet wide across which invaders would have to charge.

For centuries after the Romans left Britain, nearby farmers used stones from the wall to build fences around their fields. Many of them were crushed and used as foundation material for a new highway in the 1700s. Finally, the government acted to preserve the wall.

Hadrian's Wall has plenty of visitors but few crowds. It is relatively easy to find a section where one can walk in solitude and silence. Atop the wall, gazing north into a drizzling rain, it is easy to imagine how a soldier from sunny Italy, or perhaps even from Africa or Palestine, might have felt about defending his empire in such a bleak setting.

CHURCHES: WESTMINSTER ABBEY

There is probably no spot in England less remote than Westminster Abbey. London traffic swirls around it incessantly. The Houses of Parliament are just across the street. And yet, once a visitor is inside, the twentieth century is left behind. Certainly, it is thronged with tourists, but most are hushed and respectful. After all, this is a church and has been so for about fourteen hundred years.

The first church on the spot was built by King Saberht, first Christian king of the East Saxons, who died in 616. In 1050, Edward the Confessor dedicated his life to building what officially is the Church of St. Peter. Gradually, however,

HOW THE GARDENS GROW

Perhaps more than any other people in the world, the English love gardening. In the Middle Ages, even the poorest cottager had a small plot of land in which to raise a few vegetables and flowers. In the 1500s, formal gardens began to be laid out next to great country houses.

Knot gardens were popular in the time of Elizabeth I. These featured low hedges of boxwood or lavender pruned into intricate patterns and filled with brightly colored flowers. The Jacobean gardens of the 1600s were larger and boasted patterned terraces with fountains, statues, and topiary—bushes sculpted into geometric and animal shapes.

Gardens reached their height in the 1700s with the advent of landscape gardening. The formal, geometric gardens were replaced by more naturalized, parklike plantings. These gardens were on a grand scale, with man-made hills and ponds, bridges, and replicas of ruined Greek temples.

The English found much more than mere beauty in their gardens. They also found a place to think, reflect, and gain peace of mind. In 1712 Joseph Addison wrote:

> I look upon the Pleasure which we take in a Garden, as one of the most innocent Delights in humane Life. A Garden was the Habitation of our first Parents [Adam and Eve] before the Fall. It is naturally apt to fill the Mind with Calmness and Tranquillity, and to lay all its turbulent Passions at Rest. It gives us a great Insight into the Contrivance and Wisdom of providence, and suggests innumerable Subjects for Meditation. I cannot but think the very Complacency and Satisfaction which a Man takes in these Works of Nature, to be a laudable, if not virtuous Habit of Mind.

The English have never lost their love of gardening. Behind virtually every look-alike row house in grimy industrial towns is a small garden, the flowers of which provide rare and welcome color in an otherwise dreary setting.

it became known as the West Minster as opposed to the East Minster, St. Paul's Cathedral in London.

In 1066, William the Conqueror was crowned there. So have been every king and queen of England since, except for Edward V and Edward VIII, who were never crowned at all.

Many of the men and women who have begun their reigns in Westminster Abbey are buried there, as well. The body of Edward the Confessor lies in an elegant shrine built by Henry III, who is buried nearby. The abbey also contains, among many others, the tombs of Edward III and Henry V, heroes of the Hundred Years' War; Henry VII, first of the Tudors; and both Elizabeth I and her rival Mary, Queen of Scots.

Not only rulers but also renowned men and women from all walks of life are buried at Westminster. Two of England's greatest military heroes, Lord Nelson and the duke of Wellington, lie there. In the Poet's Corner are buried Geoffrey Chaucer and Charles Dickens. Sir Isaac Newton leads the list of scientists.

Westminster Abbey tends to overwhelm visitors with its hundreds of tombs, any one of which would be a huge attraction on its own. It also is typical of much of what one finds in England—a living, thriving church that is at the same time a monument to a thousand years of history.

CHURCHES: ST. MARTIN'S CHURCH CANTERBURY

There are no crowds, no traffic, and no noise, at the little church of St. Martin's, west of Canterbury in Kent. A sign requests visitors to turn on the lights when they enter and off when they leave. The city's great cathedral, where Thomas Becket was murdered by four of King Henry II's knights, gets most of the attention. And yet, St. Martin's is just as significant.

The building, only about eighty feet long and thirty feet wide, dates from the Roman occupation and is probably the oldest Christian church in England. Architecturally, it is nothing special, except for its age. The oldest part of the building was constructed of flat, Roman tiles sometime in the late 300s. Additions were made by both the Anglo-Saxons and Normans.

Historically, however, St. Martin's is one of the most important sites in England. It was given by the pagan King Ethelbert of Kent as a place of worship to his wife Bertha, a Christian from France, in 562. Thirty-five years later, at Bertha's urging, Ethelbert allowed the Christian monk Augustine, sent by the pope to England, to begin preaching. Eventually, Ethelbert was converted and baptized, probably in St. Martin's, and the Christianization of England had begun.

The intricately carved stone font that likely held the water with which Ethelbert was baptized still exists. It is not in a museum. It is not protected by a fence or by a glass wall. It sits in St. Martin's Church and still is used on Sundays.

CASTLES: THE TOWER OF LONDON

One would expect the most famous castle in the world to attract huge crowds, and so it does. The line to enter it is long, especially in the summer when people wait hours in the hot sun. Few people who visit England would miss the chance to see it, however, for this is the Tower of London.

Perhaps the most famous attraction in England, the Tower of London stands as a reminder of England's glorious past.

The Tower is perhaps the most well known, most visited, most famous place in all England. It has been a home to kings and a prison from which kings and queens have gone to their deaths. It has been a fortress, an armory, and even a zoo.

The Tower was begun in 1066 by William the Conqueror, who needed a safe place to live in the capital of the country he had just won in battle. He chose a spot on the north bank of the Thames River, just inside the east end of the old city wall. At the center of the complex is the White Tower, so called because it was whitewashed in 1241. The White Tower sits in the Inner Ward surrounded by two walls with nineteen towers.

Every ruler from William to James I used the Tower as a residence, although they had many others. It still is customary for English monarchs to spend the night before their coronation in the Tower.

A NONROYAL PALACE

In addition to castles and cathedrals, some of the most popular historic sites for visitors are the "stately homes," built by the nobility mostly from the 1500s through the 1700s. With the invention of gunpowder and the use of cannons, huge stone castles were no longer effective as protection against attack. Besides, they tended to be dark, dank, and drafty.

During the reign of Elizabeth I in the 1500s, great houses began to be built in such a way as to let in much more light and warmth. Windows replaced solid stone walls. Everything was designed for comfort instead of protection.

Houses grew more and more elaborate. Nobles tried to outdo one another to see who could build the most lavish estate. Such houses featured marble floors, gilded ceilings, the finest furniture, and the most splendid paintings and tapestries from Europe. It was not at all unusual for a nobleman to build himself into bankruptcy.

One of the greatest houses in England, one that rivaled even the homes of royalty, was Blenheim. After John Churchill, duke of Marlborough, won a great victory near the town of Blenheim in Germany, Queen Anne gave him the old royal manor of Woodstock a few miles north of Oxford and Parliament voted the money to build him a palace.

Blenheim Palace was designed by Sir John Vanbrugh and is considered a masterpiece of baroque architecture. It cost so much that the duke, and, after his death, his wife, had to constantly petition Parliament for more money. The grounds cover 2,700 acres and the house, 7 acres. It contains 320 rooms and features a Grand Hall with an 87-foot-high ceiling and a library 55 feet long.

Like many of England's great houses, Blenheim is so huge as to intimidate visitors. Room after room of priceless artifacts make it seem like a museum rather than a home. Such was the feeling of English poet Alexander Pope when he wrote,

"See, Sir, here's the grand approach,
This way is for his Grace's coach . . .
The council chamber's for debate,
And all the rest are rooms of state."
"Thanks, Sir," I cried, "'Tis very fine,
But where d'ye sleep and where d'ye dine?
I find by all you have been telling,
That 'tis a house but not a dwelling."

The Tower is most famous as a prison. The first prisoner was the rebellious bishop of Durham in 1100, and the last was the Nazi Rudolf Hess in 1941. Others have included Queen Elizabeth I, Sir Walter Raleigh, and the "Princes in the Tower"—twelve-year-old King Edward V and his younger brother Richard, who were probably murdered in a White Tower chamber on orders from their uncle, Richard III.

All around the Tower lies the oldest part of London, known simply as The City, now a center of banking and business. From their offices in high-rise buildings, the people who control much of England today can look toward the building that is, more than any other, a symbol of their country's past glory.

CASTLES: KENILWORTH

A few miles south of the sprawling industrial city of Birmingham is the little town of Kenilworth, outside of which is the red sandstone ruin of a great castle. Kenilworth Castle, unlike the Tower of London, is a tranquil place. Visitors can climb among the ruined buildings or walk on the grounds, envisioning how it must have appeared for a party held there more than four hundred years ago.

Kenilworth was built in the early 1100s by Geoffrey de Clinton, treasurer of King Henry I. It later became a royal castle and was used often by kings from Henry II to Henry VIII. In 1563, Elizabeth I gave Kenilworth to Robert Dudley, whom she created earl of Leicester.

In 1575, Elizabeth, who loved to travel the country, taking advantage of her subjects' hospitality, paid a nineteen-day visit to Kenilworth. Leicester went all out to impress his

The ruins of Kenilworth Castle. Built in the twelfth century, Kenilworth was a spectacular sight until its destruction during the 1649 English civil war.

queen. When she arrived and crossed the moat (an artificial river) in front of the castle, an illuminated, floating island appeared and a girl representing a water spirit welcomed Elizabeth to the castle. Tournaments were held in the daytime and banquets each night, one featuring nearly three hundred different dishes, with fireworks afterward.

Even in an age used to lavish display, Leicester's entertainment of Elizabeth made a great impression. Among those who heard all the details was eleven-year-old William Shakespeare in nearby Stratford-upon-Avon. Years later he incorporated much of the spectacle and speech into his play *A Midsummer Night's Dream.*

Little now remains of Kenilworth's glory. In 1649, during the English civil war, members of Parliament ordered it destroyed, perhaps fearing it would be a fortress used against them, perhaps hating it as a symbol of the monarchy they had come to despise.

THEATERS: THE GLOBE

Castles and cathedrals were built to last centuries. Theaters, however, were built with an eye toward economy and profit instead of durability. Despite England's great theatrical tradition, the oldest theater in the country, the Theater Royal in Bristol, dates from 1766. Several splendid theaters from the Victorian era, such as the Royal Opera House built in 1858 in London's Covent Garden, are still in use.

The most famous theaters, however, were built during the reign of Elizabeth I on the south bank of the Thames River. The Rose, the Swan, and—most famous of all—Shakespeare's Globe (1599) were built mostly of timber and roofed with straw thatch. Those that did not burn down, as the first Globe did in 1613, were torn down by the Puritans, as the second Globe was in 1644.

Visitors, however, will soon be able to see the Globe—in a way. When archaeologists uncovered the foundations of the theater in the 1970s, the late actor and director Sam Wanamaker began a campaign to have a reconstruction of the Globe built. Using drawings and written records, workers using centuries-old techniques are building a full-scale replica just a few yards from where the original stood.

In 1999, exactly four hundred years after the first Globe opened, a flag will fly over the new version announcing that

a performance will be given. Playgoers will be able to see the works of Shakespeare in much the same way their counterparts in 1600 did—some standing on the ground in front of an unadorned stage, others sitting high in the tiered boxes. The magic of Shakespeare's words and the magic of the restored theater will combine to make visitors forget that four hundred years have passed and that a second Elizabeth is on the throne.

Thanks to efforts to reconstruct the Globe Theater, theatergoers will soon be able to experience Shakespearean plays in a full-scale replica of the original theater.

History is everywhere in England. Thousands of years of buildings and barons, religion and warfare, arts and industry have left monuments that almost crowd one another in this small country. They serve as a constant reminder to the people of today of the actions and accomplishments of those who have been part of England before them.

EPILOGUE

ENGLAND'S LEGACY

History has a way of never allowing one country to monopolize center stage indefinitely. Egypt, Greece, and Rome all had their day, then passed from the spotlight. England, also, had its century as the greatest power on earth and, like the rest, stepped aside. Although England remains among the world's foremost nations, her chief contribution—like that of Greece and Rome—is the legacy she has bequeathed to others.

Many of the world's legislative bodies, including the Congress of the United States, are direct descendants of England's Parliament. The notion began in the reign of Edward I in the 1200s that the people should have a say in how they were governed. To be sure, in Edward's time and for long afterward, this meant only the nobility.

It took a bloody civil war to settle the issue, but final authority ultimately rested with Parliament, not with a monarch. Instead of rulers using Parliament to carry out their will, kings and queens came to derive their power from Parliament.

The name of the House of Commons came from the fact that members represented communities, not because they were of common birth. It was this system of government by representatives elected on a geographical basis that was to take root not only in the United States, but also in many other countries once part of the British Empire.

POLITICAL PARTIES

Rival factions have been part of government and politics since ancient times. The formalization of such groups into organized political parties developed in England as power passed from kings to Parliament.

England's political parties began when the country split into Whigs and Tories during the reign of Charles II. At first, these were little more than court factions, but they slowly grew and took on a more formal structure. Eventually, kings were forced to choose their chief ministers from among members of the party in power. From this evolved the cabinet form of government.

The importance of the political party system as it emerged in England and was later carried to England's colonies is that the parties have become the road to power. In the parliamentary system, the majority party controls the government, and the leader of the party is also the leader of the government. Only very rarely can someone rise to power outside the framework of organized political parties. This is particularly true in two-party systems such as that of the United States, where no third party has achieved any real degree of success in decades.

THE COMMON LAW

While most of Europe developed a legal tradition based on that of ancient Rome, England adopted and modified the system brought by the Anglo-Saxon invaders. Roman law depended on written codes and is now known as civil law. The English system was based instead on precedent built up over time, and came to be called the common law—the law of and defined by the community.

When a group of rebellious barons forced King John to sign a document known as the Magna Carta (great charter) in 1215, their position was that longstanding custom and tradition could not be overturned, even by a king. This doctrine, applied to legal matters, defined the law in terms of what had been the accepted custom. By 1297, courts had been given the name "common law," and "year books" were compiled giving details of cases.

The legal system of England and many of her former possessions, including the United States, is based on common law. Court decisions are not based on written codes so much as on how previous courts have ruled in similar cases. The advantage of such a system is that the law has been allowed to grow, evolve, and adapt to new and different circumstances.

THE JURY SYSTEM

In the Europe of a thousand years ago, people often had to face death or injury in order to prove their innocence. A

Rebellious barons force King John to sign the Magna Carta, which enforced the use of long-standing custom as a legal basis. By the end of the thirteenth century, the English legal system implemented common law, or law based on precedent.

person accused of a crime might be subjected to trial by ordeal. If a red-hot iron touched to his tongue burned him, he was guilty. Two knights on opposite sides of a legal question would often meet in trial by combat. The theory in both cases was that God would protect the innocent and reveal the guilty.

As the legal system grew more complex, a better system of deciding cases was needed. Under William the Conqueror and his successors, royal judges were sent throughout the country to settle land disputes. They occasionally would assemble a body of witnesses from which they would get the facts of a case. The Assize of Clarendon in 1166 established a system whereby a "jury of presentment" consisting of twelve "lawful" men would be gathered to swear before a judge as to a person's guilt or innocence.

Over the next one hundred years, the jury system underwent a dramatic change. Instead of being composed of those already acquainted with the facts of a case, juries were made up of people who knew nothing about it and would render a decision based on the arguments of both sides.

The jury system provided a fair and efficient method of dispensing justice. It also had the effect of increasing participation by the people in government. The tradition of one's guilt or innocence decided by one's fellow citizens, instead of by a judge or panel of judges, has passed from England to much of the rest of the world.

THE ANGLICAN CHURCH

When King Henry VIII broke with the pope in 1533 over the question of his marriage, he had no intention of starting a separate church, but that is what happened. What Henry wanted to be the Catholic Church *in* England became the Church *of* England that eventually developed worldwide into the Anglican Church.

Wherever England planted colonies throughout the world, the Church of England went also. At first, the

Henry VIII's break with the pope in 1533 led to the formation of the Anglican Church.

church's bishops were under the jurisdiction of the archbishop of Canterbury, head of the Church of England, just as the colonists were under the control of Parliament. As the colonies won or were given their independence, however, the churches became national in character. The Church of England became the Episcopal Church in the United States, for instance. Others include the Churches of South Africa, Canada, and Kenya. Other churches, such as those in Japan and China, were formed through the efforts of missionaries. In 1996, there were approximately 90 million members of Anglican churches worldwide.

Unlike the Catholic Church, the Anglican Communion—the name given to all the Church of England and its offspring—does not have a central authority. Some countries have several archbishops. Some have only one. Some have none. The Episcopal Church of the United States, for instance, has a "presiding bishop," but power rests with individual bishops in their geographical areas, called dioceses. The only things linking the members of the Anglican Communion are tradition and identical or very similar forms of services.

The Anglican Church grew out of the typical desire of the English to find a middle ground between two extremes. The position of the church and its tradition of tolerance has enabled it to be effective in promoting dialogue among various Christian churches and among the various religions of the world.

THE ENGLISH LANGUAGE

Perhaps the most outstanding contribution of England to the world has been its language. This combination of Anglo-Saxon, Scandinavian, and Norman-French has grown from a language spoken only by the peasants of a backward island nation to the one most understood throughout the world.

England's contributions in the visual arts, such as painting and sculpture, and in music cannot compare with those of France, Italy, Germany, China, and many others. No country, however, has a richer history of drama and literature. From the tales of Geoffrey Chaucer

Geoffrey Chaucer

to the plays of William Shakespeare to the novels of Charles Dickens and Sir Walter Scott to the poetry of Rudyard Kipling to the speeches of Winston Churchill, the English have used their language to stir the hearts and imaginations of the world.

Wherever they planted their flag, the English took their language. As a result, it became the predominant language of the United States, Canada, and Australia. In other countries, such as India or South Africa, people from tribes or regions with different languages could usually talk to one another in English.

As the twentieth century draws to a close, English is fast becoming the international language. From Japan to Mexico, students normally study their own language first, English second. It is the official language of international air travel and the unofficial language of international business.

In the 1800s, the English could say with pride, "The sun never sets on the British Empire." This was literally true. So vast were England's possessions that, at every time of day, the sun was shining on a British flag somewhere on the face of the globe. The twentieth century, with two world wars and a depression, brought sunset to the British Empire, but the light of England's contributions to civilization can never be extinguished.

The eloquent speeches of Winston Churchill have inspired millions of people around the world.

FACTS ABOUT ENGLAND

(Asterisk indicates statistics are for United Kingdom, including England, Scotland, Wales, Northern Ireland)

COMPARATIVE POPULATION

Year	England and Wales	London	Other English Cities
A.D. 200	1,000,000	20,000	York, 20,000
1100	1,500,000	15,000	York, 9,000 Lincoln, 4,000 Oxford, 4,000 Norwich, 4,000
1400	2,250,000	45,000	York, 11,000 Bristol, 9,000
1500	3,000,000	75,000	York, 20,000 Norwich, 15,000 Bristol, 15,000
1600	4,500,000	220,000	York, 20,000 Norwich, 20,000
1700	6,000,000	575,000	Bristol, 30,000 Norwich, 29,000
1800	8,890,000	1,117,000	Liverpool, 382,000 Manchester, 338,000 Birmingham, 233,000
1850	17,983,000	2,685,000	Liverpool, 376,000 Manchester, 338,000 Birmingham, 233,000
1900	32,612,000	6,586,000	Liverpool, 704,000 Manchester, 645,000 Birmingham, 523,000
1950	43,758,000	8,193,000	Birmingham, 1,113,000 Liverpool, 789,000 Manchester, 703,000
1975	49,184,000	7,027,000	Birmingham, 1,062,000 Leeds, 774,000 Sheffield, 555,000 Liverpool, 542,000 Manchester, 496,000
1992 (est.)	49,650,000	6,904,000	Birmingham, 1,009,000 Leeds, 721,000 Sheffield, 531,000 Liverpool, 479,000 Bradford, 477,000 Manchester, 434,000

PEOPLE*

Total population (1991): 58,090,000 (England only, 47,800,000)

Average years of school, females over 25 (1990): 11.5; world rank, 3rd

Average years of school, males over 25 (1990): 11.4; world rank, 8th

Percentage of females with postsecondary education (1989): 8 percent; world rank, 18th

Percentage of males with postsecondary education (1989): 11.9 percent; world rank, 22nd

Rooms per household (1982): 4.8; world rank, 9th

Percentage of households with (1992): automobiles, 68 percent; telephones, 88 percent; televisions, 98 percent; refrigerators, 99 percent; central heat, 82 percent; washing machines, 88 percent

Percentage of households headed by women (1991): 25 percent; world rank, 17th

Percentage of labor force in (1991): agriculture, 2 percent; industry, 29 percent; services, 68 percent

Comparative life expectancy: 1955, 68.2 years; 1965, 70.8 years; 1975, 72 years; 1985, 74 years; 1995, 76.2 years (world rank, 16th)

Annual population growth rate (1995): .24 percent; world rank, 154th

Population density per square kilometer (1995): 238; world rank, 20th

Population over 65 (1995): 9,036,000; world rank, 8th

Population under 15 (1995): 11,460,000; world rank, 28th

Birth rate per 1,000 population (1992): 13.5 (world average, 26.0)

Death rate per 1,000 population (1992): 10.9 (world average, 9.2)

Percentage of population in cities over 750,000: 1955, 29.9 percent; 1965, 28.3 percent; 1975, 25.8 percent; 1985, 23.6 percent; 1995, 23 percent (world rank, 45th)

Ethnicity (1991): Anglo, 94.2 percent; Asian Indian, 1.4 percent; Pakistani, 0.9 percent; West Indian, 0.8 percent; African, 0.3 percent; Chinese, 0.3 percent; Bangladeshi, 0.2 percent

Religious affiliation (8.4 million active members), 1990: Christian, 80 percent (Roman Catholic, 21 percent; Anglican, 20 percent; Presbyterian, 14 percent; Methodist, 5 percent; Baptist, 3 percent; other 37 percent); Muslim, 11 percent; Sikh, 4 percent; Hindu, 2 percent; Jewish, 1 percent

LAND*

Land area: 94,555 square miles (England only, 50,363 square miles)

Highest point (England): Scafell Pike, 3,210 feet

Lowest point (England): The Fens, East Anglia, sea level

Longest rivers (England): Thames, 215 miles; Severn, 210 miles; Trent, 170 miles

Natural forest: 8,254 square miles

Pasture land: 44,285 square miles

Municipal waste: 18,000,000 metric tons per year

Oil exports: 1971, 25,330 metric tons; 1981, 53,720 metric tons; 1991, 119,400 metric tons

Hard coal reserves: 5,665,000 metric tons (1991)

Soft coal reserves: 43.96 metric tons (1991)

CLIMATE (THAMES RIVER VALLEY)

	April	July	October	January
Average high temperature (Fahrenheit)	56	71	58	44
Average low temperature (Fahrenheit)	40	54.5	44	34
Hours of sunshine daily	5.5	6	3	1.5
Average monthly rainfall (in inches)	1.6	2.2	2.5	2.4

ECONOMY*

(All monetary figures in U.S. dollars)

Per capita government expenditures: $5,043; world rank, 17th

Percent of government expenditures (1989): defense, 12.46 percent (world rank, 29th); education, 2.94 percent (world rank, 91st)

Imports (1993): $203.1 billion (machinery and transportation equipment, 39.2 percent; road vehicles, 10.6 percent; chemical products, 9.5 percent; food products, 9.9 percent; petroleum products, 4.2 percent; textiles, 2.9 percent; metals, 2.9 percent; paper, 2.8 percent; iron and steel products, 1.9 percent; others, 16.1 percent.

Exports (1992): $177.7 billion (machinery and transportation equipment, 40.7 percent; chemical products, 14.5 percent; road vehicles, 7.0 percent; petroleum products, 6.6 percent; scientific instruments, 4.0 percent; iron and steel products, 2.6 percent; clothing, 2.3 percent; others, 22.3 percent)

Gross national product: 1970, $122 billion; 1980, $449 billion; 1992, $1,025 billion (world rank, 6th)

Per capita gross national product: 1970, $2,210; 1980, $7,980; 1992, $17,770 (world rank, 17th)

CHRONOLOGY

B.C.

ca. 2200
Building of Stonehenge begins

ca. 700
Celtic tribes begin invasion of Britain

55–54
Britain invaded by Romans led by Julius Caesar

A.D.

43
Second Roman invasion establishes Britain as Roman colony

410
Roman troops withdrawn

ca. 450
Angles, Saxons, Jutes begin invasion of Britain

597
Augustine converts King Ethelbert of Kent, becomes first archbishop of Canterbury

789
Vikings from Denmark and Norway begin raiding England

878
King Alfred of Wessex defeats Danes at Battle of Edington

937
Athelstan becomes first king of a united England

1013
Invasion of England by King Sweyn Forkbeard of Denmark

1017
Canute becomes first Danish king of England

1050
Edward the Confessor begins building of Westminster Abbey

1066
William, duke of Normandy, defeats King Harold of England at Battle of Hastings, becomes first of Norman kings

1135

Civil war begins when King Henry I dies without an heir

1154

Henry II, son of Count Geoffrey of Anjou, becomes king of England and ruler of Angevin empire

1166

Assize of Clarendon establishes jury system

1167

English scholars, banned from University of Paris, begin to settle in Oxford

1170

Archbishop Thomas Becket murdered in Canterbury cathedral by four of Henry II's knights

1215

Rebellious barons force King John to sign Magna Carta

1249

First Oxford college, University College, founded

1282

King Edward I conquers Wales

1295

Edward I summons first representative English Parliament

1337

King Edward III claims throne of France; Hundred Years' War with France begins

1346

Edward III defeats French at Crécy; English occupy Calais

1349–1351

Plague known as Black Death kills one-third of population of England

1356

Edward the Black Prince defeats French at Poitiers

1381

Peasants' Revolt

1387

Geoffrey Chaucer begins writing *The Canterbury Tales*

1415

King Henry V defeats French at Agincourt

1453

French defeat English at Battle of Castillon; end of Hundred Years' War

1455
Wars of the Roses between houses of Lancaster and York begin

1485
Henry Tudor defeats King Richard III at Battle of Bosworth Field, becomes King Henry VII, first Tudor monarch

1497
John Cabot becomes first English explorer to visit the New World

1534
King Henry VIII breaks with Catholic Church

1535
Henry VIII seizes all property of Catholic Church in England

1549
First Church of England *Book of Common Prayer* written by Thomas Cranmer

1558
Elizabeth I becomes queen; Elizabethan Settlement secures religious peace

1577
Sir Francis Drake embarks on voyage around the world

1585
First English colony in the New World established at Roanoke, Virginia

1588
English navy defeats Spanish Armada

1592
William Shakespeare's first play, *Henry VI*, performed

1600
East India Company founded

1603
Elizabeth I dies and is succeeded by James I, first Stuart king

1611
King James Version of Bible published

1642
Civil war between King Charles I and Parliament begins

1649
Charles I executed; period of English Commonwealth begins

1660

Monarchy restored by Charles II

1666

Great Fire destroys much of London

1678

First political parties, Whigs and Tories, formed

1688

Glorious Revolution ousts James II and brings William of Orange to throne

1690

Battle of Boyne begins dominance of English Protestants in Northern Ireland

1704

John Churchill, duke of Marlborough, defeats French at Blenheim

1707

Act of Union unites England and Scotland

1713

Treaty of Utrecht gives England Gibraltar, Minorca, Nova Scotia, and Newfoundland

1714

Queen Anne dies; George I becomes first Hanoverian king

1721

Sir Robert Walpole becomes England's first prime minister

1738

John Wesley begins preaching doctrine known as Methodism

1746

Last Stuart claimant to throne, "Bonnie Prince Charlie," defeated at Culloden

1763

Peace of Paris ends Seven Years' War; England gets all of Canada and control of much of India

1776

American colonies declare independence

1782

James Watt invents the steam engine, signaling start of Industrial Revolution

1783

England gives up American colonies in Treaty of Paris

1788
English colony established in Australia

1805
English navy under Lord Nelson defeats French at Battle of Trafalgar

1815
Duke of Wellington defeats French under Napoléon Bonaparte at Waterloo; Peace of Vienna gives England Cape Colony, Ceylon, and Guiana

1829
Sir Robert Peel creates first English police force, known as "bobbies" in his honor; Act of Emancipation gives full civil rights to Catholics

1832
Reform Bill reallocates seats in Parliament; all male property owners given right to vote

1833
Slavery outlawed in British Empire

1837
Victoria becomes queen, opening longest reign in English history

1851
Charles Dickens writes *David Copperfield*

1867
Second Reform Bill gives vote to small farmers, city workers

1870
Education Act establishes first state schools; school made compulsory for all children to age eleven

1888
Local Government Act establishes county councils

1899–1902
England fights Dutch settlers in Boer War in South Africa

1900
Labour Party founded

1903
Suffragettes begin demanding voting rights for women

1914–1918
World War I

1919

Vote given to women over thirty

1921

Ireland divided into Irish Free State in the south and Ulster in the north

1928

Vote given to all men and women over twenty-one

1931

Great Depression hits England

1939

World War II begins; England declares war on Germany

1940

Winston Churchill becomes prime minister; Royal Air Force defeats German Luftwaffe in Battle of Britain

1948

National Health Service established

1953

Elizabeth II crowned in Westminster Abbey

1957

India and Pakistan gain independence; immigration from Caribbean begins

1963

Beatles become top-rated musical group

1973

England joins European Economic Community

1975

Oil drilling begins in North Sea

1982

England defeats Argentina in war over Falkland Islands

1994

Tunnel under English Channel links England and France

Suggestions for Further Reading

Clifford Lindsey Alderman, *The Golden Century: England Under the Tudors*. New York: Julian Messner, 1972. An excellent background to Elizabeth I's reign. Good opening chapter on the contributions of the Tudors.

Catherine M. Andronik, *Searching for the Real King Arthur*. New York: Atheneum, 1989. Traces the legends of the Anglo-Saxon hero from the standpoints of both literature and archaeology. Illustrations and photos.

Richard W. Barber, *England in the Middle Ages*. New York: Seabury Press, 1976. Good overview of both the political and social history of England during the Middle Ages.

Janice Young Brooks, *Kings and Queens: The Plantagenets of England*. Nashville: Thomas Nelson, 1975. A lively telling of the lives and times of the Plantagenets, who ruled England from 1153 until 1485.

Olivia Coolidge, *Winston Churchill and the Story of Two World Wars*. Boston: Houghton Mifflin, 1960. Despite the title, this is a complete biography of the famous prime minister, although the sections on the world wars take up the most space (130 pages for World War II alone). Good maps showing the various theaters of war.

Kevin Crossley-Holland, *Green Blades Rising*. New York: Seabury Press, 1975. Description of life in Anglo-Saxon England for older readers. Good photographs, mostly black-and-white.

S. E. Ellacott, *The Norman Invasion*. London: Abelard-Schuman, 1966. The history of England from the reign of Canute through the Norman Conquest. Well-written summary for older children. Excellent black-and-white illustrations.

David Flint, *The United Kingdom.* Austin, TX: Raintree Steck-Vaughn Publishers, 1994. Part of Country Fact Files series. Overview of life in the United Kingdom is especially good in that graphs and charts appear on every page.

Carol Greene, *England.* Chicago: Childrens Press, 1982. Excellent survey of the geography, history, and everyday life of England. One of the few available that concentrates on England rather than the entire United Kingdom. Short biographies of major figures such as Sir Francis Drake, Florence Nightingale are a good touch.

Ian James, *Inside Great Britain.* London: Franklin Watts, 1988. Short book with ten sections dealing with various aspects of life in Great Britain. Color photographs.

Gerald W. Johnson, *The British Empire.* New York: Morrow and Company, 1969. Intended for American students whose knowledge of English history stops at 1776. Covers the rise and fall of the British Empire, including short biographies of empire builders such as Clive of India and Rhodes of South Africa.

Robin May, *Alfred the Great and the Saxons.* Hove, England: Wayland Publishers, 1984. Gives the history, not only of the reign of Alfred, but also of the Anglo-Saxon invasion from the beginning up to the Norman Conquest. Special attention to social life. Color illustrations and some photos.

Amanda Purves, *Growing Up in a Saxon Village.* Hove, England: Wayland Publishers Ltd., 1978. Looks at life in Anglo-Saxon England from the standpoints of family, home life, school, work and play, religion, and warfare. Very easy to read.

R. R. Sellman, *Norman England.* New York: Roy Publishers, 1959. Account of the Norman invasion and the Battle of Hastings, plus a great deal on the subsequent changes in England, including the imposition of the feudal system. Good black-and-white illustrations. For older children.

Anna Sproule, *Great Britain.* New York: Bookwright Press, 1988. Part of Countries of the World series. Twenty short sections on various aspects of Great Britain from wildlife to industry. Plenty of color photographs throughout.

Jetty St. John, *A Family in England*. Minneapolis, MN: Lerner Publications, 1988. Interesting approach in that life in England is described in terms of a single family living in a Cambridgeshire village—their work, schools, leisure.

R. J. Unstead, *Invaded Island: A Pictorial History, Stone Age to 1066*. London: Macdonald and Company, 1971. Excellent general history of Britain and England. Lavishly illustrated with color drawings, photos, and maps.

Sylvia Wright, *The Age of Chivalry: English Society 1200–1400*. New York: Warwick Press, 1988. Well-illustrated social and political history of England in the Middle Ages.

WORKS CONSULTED

R. J. C. Atkinson, *Stonehenge and Avebury.* Swindon, England: Swindon Press, 1959. Written by a professor of archaeology who has done extensive work at both sites, this is one of the most complete guidebooks available to any site or monument in England. Especially interesting are the aerial views of present-day Stonehenge and Avebury alongside an artist's renderings of how they used to appear.

John Birley, *Housesteads.* Newcastle upon Tyne, England: Frank Graham Publishers, 1973. Detailed description of the ruins of the best-preserved fort along Hadrian's Wall. Especially interesting artist's conception of how fort looked in the second century A.D. Complete with bibliography.

Kathleen Campbell, *Sarah, Duchess of Marlborough.* London: Thornton Butterworth, 1932. Thorough biography of the woman whose influence on Queen Anne so affected English history. Long paragraphs and sentences and lack of photographs make for a somewhat dull read.

Christopher Donaldson, *St. Martin's Church Canterbury.* Ramsgate, England: The Church Publishers, 1966. Charming guidebook tells not only the history, but also some of the legends surrounding this ancient church. The author was the church's rector (supervising priest) at the time the book was written.

Adam Fox, *Westminster Abbey.* London: Pitkin Pictorials, 1975. This guidebook to Westminster Abbey, written by a Church of England official, dwells more on the religious aspects of the abbey than most. Good color photographs.

David Frost and Antony Jay, *The English.* New York: Stein and Day, 1968. A largely irreverent and cynical look at how the lives and outlook of the English have changed since World War II, especially the revolution in dress and behavior of young people in the 1960s.

Anthony Glynn, *The British: Portrait of a People*. New York: G. P. Putnam's Sons, 1970. A lighthearted but sometimes pointed look at life in Great Britain. The numerous short chapters deal with everything from religion to pubs.

F. E. Halliday, *England: A Concise History*. London: Thames and Hudson, 1989. Very good overview of English history, well illustrated with more than two hundred drawings, photographs, and maps.

Christopher Hibbert, *The English: A Social History, 1066-1945*. New York: W. W. Norton, 1987. Delightfully written and sprinkled throughout with contemporary quotations. Examines all aspects of life in England in four different eras: medieval, Tudor-Renaissance, Hanoverian, Victorian to the present.

P. K. Ballie Reynolds, *Kenilworth Castle*. Edinburgh, Scotland: Her Majesty's Stationery Office Press, 1975. Small pamphlet describing the history and architecture of the castle. Good diagram showing which parts were built when, but no photographs.

T. H. Rowland, *Short Guide to the Roman Wall*. Newcastle upon Tyne, England: Frank Graham Publishers, 1973. Excellent guidebook describing the building and history of Hadrian's Wall. Ideal for the tourist in that it gives section-by-section guides to what to see along the wall.

A. L. Rowse, *The Tower of London in the History of England*. New York: G. P. Putnam's Sons, 1982. Meticulously documented and well-illustrated history of the Tower from its building under William the Conqueror to present times.

J. D. Scott, *Life in Britain*. New York: William Morrow, 1956. Examination of life in Great Britain. Chapters deal with geography, education, government, the media, law, and social life. Interesting, but much information is dated.

Alicia Street, *The Land and People of England*. Philadelphia: J. B. Lippincott, 1969. One volume in a large series from this publisher on various countries around the world. Opening chapters deal with geographical information and most of the remainder is divided between history and a look at contemporary English life.

Lawrence E. Tanner, *Westminster Abbey*. London: Pitkin Pictorials, 1968. The history and architectural description of Westminster Abbey in a guidebook with plenty of color and black-and-white photographs.

Paul Theroux, *The Kingdom by the Sea: A Journey Around Great Britain*. Boston: Houghton Mifflin, 1983. An American author looks at and reflects on life in Great Britain during a three-month trip around the coastline. A penetrating, pessimistic view of the British.

————, *This is Bath*. Bath, England: Unichrome, 1993. This guidebook to Bath contains text in three languages (English, German, French) and many color pictures of the city's sites. Good history and description of Roman ruins.

Eric Thomas and John T. White, *Hedgerow*. New York: William Morrow, 1980. Gorgeously illustrated book is intended for children and yet is an interesting and thorough study of this English phenomenon.

George M. Trevelyan, *History of England*. Garden City, NY: Doubleday, 1953. A must for any serious student of English history, this three-volume work is also well written enough to entertain the casual reader. Author excels at explaining the impact of events in addition to describing them.

James Turner, *Sceptered Isle: The Countryside of Britain*. New York: Methuen Publications, 1977. Chapters deal with various aspects of the landscape of Great Britain: lakes, mountains, moors, the coast. Well illustrated with photographs, mostly black-and-white.

Derek Wilson, *The Tower*. New York: Charles Scribner's Sons, 1979. A thorough history of the Tower of London but not nearly as well illustrated as Rowse's version.

INDEX

Picture Credits

Cover photo: FPG International
Archive Photos, 8, 12, 13, 20, 28, 86, 88 (top), 94, 99
Archive Photos/American Stock, 59
Archive Photos/Express Newspapers, 78
Archive Photos/IMAPRESS, 89
Archive Photos/Nancy Nugent, 85
Archive Photos/Popperfoto, 22
Archive Photos/Press Association, 101
The Bettmann Archive, 27
©Dan Budnik/Woodfin Camp & Associates, Inc., 77
Corbis-Bettmann, 40, 43, 80
©Dick Durrance/Woodfin Camp & Associates, Inc., 90
©Anthony Howarth/Woodfin Camp & Associates, Inc., 15
©Hulton Getty/Woodfin Camp & Associates, Inc., 75, 82
Library of Congress, 25, 32, 42, 44, 45, 46, 61, 62, 64, 106
National Archives, 70, 107
North Wind Picture Archives, 41, 49, 50, 104, 105
Reuters/Bettmann, 81
©Paul Solomon/Woodfin Camp & Associates, Inc., 16
©Bob Straus/Woodfin Camp & Associates, Inc., 11, 73
©Homer Sykes/Woodfin Camp & Associates, Inc., 35
Donald M. Witte, *Photo Archive of Famous Places of the World*, published by Dover Publications, Inc., 92, 97
©Adam Woolfitt/Woodfin Camp & Associates, Inc., 21, 88 (bottom), 93

About the Author

William W. Lace is a native of Fort Worth, Texas. He holds a bachelor's degree from Texas Christian University, a master's from East Texas State University, and a doctorate from the University of North Texas. After working for newspapers in Baytown, Texas, and Fort Worth, he joined the University of Texas at Arlington as sports information director and later became the director of the news service. He is now vice chancellor for public affairs at Tarrant County Junior College in Fort Worth. He and his wife, Laura, live in Arlington and have two children. Lace's other books include biographies of baseball player Nolan Ryan, artist Michelangelo, and statesman Winston Churchill, and histories of the Hundred Years' War and Elizabethan England.